D0110999

# By the Light of the Moon

### Reflections on Wholeness of Being

## Bunny McBride

Copyright © 2014 Bunny McBride

All rights reserved.

ISBN-13: 978-0615954431 (Custom)
ISBN-10: 061595443X

Wisbee Creek Press
Bath, Maine

Wisbee Creek Press

For my sister, Susan

# CONTENTS

# ACKNOWLEDGMENTS

These essays come from a wellspring of gratitude, beginning with thanks for Australian essayist Neil Millar, who guided me into this genre so many years ago, followed by *Christian Science Monitor* Home Forum Page editor Henrietta Buckmaster, who published those early pieces, and my husband Harald Prins, who prodded me to return to essay writing. Special thanks to friends who read this new collection and pressed me to share it beyond our close circle – Phyllis Austin, Lucas Bessire, Kelly Mae Jensen, Pierre Pradervand, Lisa Redfern, Lark Rodman, Pam Spaulding, Denise Wyrick, and the "Ropeholders": Ruth Ann Wefald, Peg Hornsby, Beth Kesinger, Kristin Miller, and Linda Cates. And, most of all, gratitude to my sister, Susan McBride Els, a tiller of soil and prose, who watered and weeded all of these pages, and graces some of them with her presence.

# INTRODUCTION: NOTICING THE MOON

*And the darkness shall be the light.* ~T.S. Eliot

The earliest memory I have of the moon is on a hot summer night when I was about six. My father came into the bedroom I shared with my sister to check on us. Restless in the heat, we asked for water. Our twin beds were positioned alongside adjacent walls, with a window at the foot end of each bed. After giving us a drink, Dad turned his attention to the windowpanes, opening them as high as they could go and folding the curtains up over their rods. To help us catch the faint breeze, he wiped our foreheads with a cool damp facecloth, followed by a kiss. Then, wishing us sweet dreams, he left the room.

I think it was my sister's idea to turn ourselves upside down in our beds so we could put our pillows on the window sills and press our noses against the screens for a bit more air. As I breathed in deeply, I saw it: A full moon pressed against a black sky. It looked like the bottom of a cool glass of milk.

After that, I noticed the moon often, intrigued by its many incarnations: a balloon caught in a tree, a circle of light at the end of a tunnel, the universe mouthing "O!", a raised eyebrow, a silver canoe gliding through clouds, a crescent hook where one could hang dreams. . . Whatever its shape and my imaginings, it became a true companion—and sometimes a guide on *how* to companion: When the moon and I are both up late in the same place, it never fails to walk me all the way home; it brightens my darkest nights and listens without saying a word; countless times, it has pulled me to the shore of solace and then slipped quietly away; when it leaves, I can count on it returning; no matter what shape it's in, whether waxing or waning, it expresses light; and rather than claim all the attention with all that light, it shines on others, making them glow.

The essays on these pages celebrate such moonly qualities. All of them, in one way or another, feature the moon. They're presented in four parts: *Writing with the Moon* relays the genesis of the essays. *At Home with the Moon* features stories situated in places where I have lived. *Traveling with the Moon* tells of far-away experiences on another continent—Africa. *Mending with the Moon* is comprised of essays having to do with various kinds of healing, especially grief.

Part parable, part memoir, the essays reveal a life of relative privilege, for I grew up in a family where love, trust, and security seemed guaranteed. But my life, like everyone else's, presented its own particular difficulties. They ranged from a long struggle with epilepsy to the heartbreak of divorce, the ordeals of a near death experience, late-term miscarriages, chronic pain, and the loss of loved ones. Some of the essays touch on those experiences, but hardship is not the thread that ties them together. Inspired by the moon, they are, at heart, about what happens when we search for and give our attention to the light within us and others, even when it is cloaked in darkness.

I wrote them on a small offshore island during a 10-week, self-imposed exile, aimed at rediscovering balance after four intense years of caring for my elderly father. A newly orphaned adult with no family members left in the generations above mine, I had come to an unprecedented chapter in my life and felt the need to recalibrate priorities and purpose. Like so many in my own generation, I was at a point of transition. I wanted it to be meaningful and graceful.

My hermitage was a little house near the sea. Arriving there with weary heart, mind, and body, I spent the first day clearing out the rental cottage as if trying to empty my head. I pared it down to essentials, removing curtains, wall art, knickknacks, and much of the furniture from the living areas to a storage room. What remained were light and space.

In the weeks that followed, I fell into a welcome rhythm: sleeping eight hours a night, rising early, starting each day with spiritual exploration/prayer/meditation, followed by yoga and six hours of writing. At the end of my work day, I biked to the local pool to do laps. Every evening at sunset, I took a long beach walk that often lasted until the sky turned dark and the stars arrived. In bed at night, I fell asleep listening to the pulse of the sea. Frequently, I awoke in the wee hours, and the ocean's voice would beckon me outside. I would sit in my "moon chair" on the patio and gaze up at the sky, or pull my jeans on over my nightgown and walk down to the beach.

One night, surrounded by the shore's vast spaciousness and accompanied by my moon shadow, I found myself thinking about unanticipated collateral blessings born of laboring through hardships. Epilepsy had prompted a dedication to attentiveness that remained with me after the illness finally disappeared. Surviving near death had transformed my sense of life, infusing it with the power of gratitude and dispelling any fear of dying. Divorce had taught me the importance of clear communication and how to hold loved ones in a larger and looser embrace. Qualities of motherhood awakened during pregnancies that ended too soon had found expression within a cherished circle of other people's children. And the recent passing of my parents had offered a new and unexpected bond with countless others adjusting to the loss of their elders. . . *There is light in the night*, I thought, glancing up at the moon.

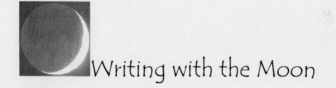Writing with the Moon

Bunny McBride

## THE MOON REMAINS

*I have never missed the full moon or the slipper of its coming back.*

~Mary Oliver

I was flying to Washington, DC, to see my surviving parent. My father had lost his wife, my mother, half a year before their 60th wedding anniversary. Almost invariably, condolence messages included the words vibrant, laughter, joy, enthusiasm. He missed the company of her dawn-to-dark vitality. I missed her voice—the lively "Hello!" with which she always answered the phone and the expectant "Tell me what's happening" that followed.

When the plane reached cruising altitude, I pulled out my computer and placed it on the tray table, intending to work during the 3-hour trip. But instead of opening it, I closed my eyes. Memories of early childhood flights with my parents came to mind—back in the 1950s when people still dressed up for what was then a very special way to travel. Beautiful stewardesses wearing perky hats and heels were always kind to my sister and me, attaching wing pins to our smocked dresses. One time they gave us a basket of Chiclets and invited us to walk up and down the aisles to deliver the candy-coated gum to passengers. We were proud working girls, quite certain everyone believed we were real, if rather small, stewardesses.

My thoughts roamed through an array of filmic recollections of our family life. The reels, mostly sweet, happy, and outdoors, seemed endless: picnicking at dawn surrounded by birdsong and dappled light; combing the woods behind our house for seedlings to transplant in our yard; swimming and ice skating at the lake; racing the wind on our bikes; red cheeks in winter, brown skin in summer, tough bare feet. Nothing extraordinary, except, perhaps, the amount of time we spent together, the possibility of watching my father on television, and the fact that we rarely missed being at the same table for dinner.

But now there was no one at Dad's table. This was his choice. He had declined invitations to live with my sister or me, preferring to inhabit the space that held echoes of his life partner. It saddened me to think of him living alone for long stretches of time until either my sister or I flew in to see him every six weeks or so. Looking for some lightness of being in the hope of greeting him with a bit of the joy he was missing, I slipped my laptop back into its bag and retrieved a book.

I'd read Dean Sluyter's *The Zen Commandments* before and always intended to visit it again. A playfully contemplative exploration of kindness, freedom and bliss, it focuses on the inner awareness from which outward behavior springs. I flipped through the pages, reading passages I'd underlined and notes I'd made in the margins. Then, coming to page 124, an unmarked poem caught my eye. Something written by the Zen hermit Ryokan upon returning to his tiny hut and finding that a thief had made off with his few possessions:

> The thief left it there
> in the window frame—
> the shining moon.

I'd breezed past this haiku in my first read, but this time it arrested my thought. Years earlier, while attending graduate school in New York and living in a cheap 5th-floor walk-up apartment, I too, came home and discovered a robbery. The thief had climbed up the back alley fire escape under the cover of night, shoved open an unlocked window and ransacked the place. Little was missing because there was so little to take that had any monetary value. Still, my apartment mate and I felt shaken and violated—and foolish for not locking the window. Closing it, I noticed the moon hanging above the alley and paused at its beauty. I remember feeling heartened by it. But, unlike Ryokan, I didn't write a poem.

Now, sitting on the plane, thinking back on that experience in light of Ryokan's words, I saw the poem as a reminder that the most precious elements of life cannot be stolen. The moon is always there, even when out of sight. And a mother's love, once given, is a constant presence that can be called up for solace whether she's in the room or not. It takes practice to realize this in everyday life, but it is a healing and gratifying goal.

On the heels of this thought came a flood of images: visual recollections of events, experiences, moments of meaning in which I was conscious of the moon's presence as witness or catalyst. I began writing them down on the fly leaves of Sluyter's book. By the time my plane landed in D.C., I had a scrawled inventory of forty recollections—seeds for the essays in this book.

I greeted my father with joy that day, feeling my mother's presence the moment I entered their home.

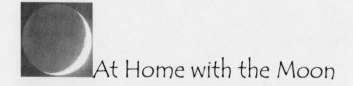At Home with the Moon

Bunny McBride

## MERCY TRAIN

*The moon, like to a silver bow new-bent in heaven,*
*Shall behold the night of our solemnities.* ~ William Shakespeare

Midnight, mid-winter, New York City. An ice-shard moon slit the hard, dark sky, while mean cold sliced through the seams of my thick woolen coat and weaseled through the pores of my leather gloves. I'd spent the evening in the university library, and now, racing against clock and arctic air, pressing book bag to chest, I ran to board the subway. The Red Line: It stretched from Harlem, through the city's Upper West Side where I went to graduate school, and down toward the Lower East Side where I lived in a bedraggled walk-up apartment that offered me little comfort as I wrestled with the loss of my first husband. As I sat down, my eyes began to burn with the sudden switch from night's bitter wind to the warm, stale air in the brightly lit train.

Like all New York subways, the Red Line usually carries a thousand themes of humanity. But not at this late hour. Tonight, in this particular car, it carried just one man— and me.

The train had screeched through a half dozen stops

before I really took notice of him, slumped over in a seat kitty-corner to me. He wore a cumbersome gray-blue coat ventilated with a dozen holes, belted with rags. Legs sprawled, head hanging forward, a mass of wooly black hair hiding his face. His right arm clutched two bulky bags, propped beside him and cushioning him like kind old ladies. The other arm hung limp between his knees, long thick fingers dangling wearily. Safety pins secured the seams of his thin green trousers—trousers that hung short of bare ankles swollen and chapped by winter air. Tie shoes, lacking laces and too big in size, encased his sockless feet.

My heart went out to this survivor who had apparently come to the subway for heat and rest, and who was now, almost contentedly, sucking wisps of warm air into his throat. As I listened to his low snore, I wondered what sort of jolt in life's journey had brought him here. Although I couldn't see his face, I recognized something about this man, as if we'd met, perhaps in what were better times for both of us. I saw in him a heartrending magnification of my own struggle to survive the harsher chapters of life. I marveled at his durability. Clearly, his tribulations were seismic compared to mine. I tried to imagine what it was like to seek solace in a subway.

I don't know how long I stared at him, but suddenly I became aware that the train was approaching my stop. I looked at his pathetic shoes and then down at my own booted feet, knowing that under those boots was a layer of jeans and under those jeans a double padding of wool socks. Socks never seemed so important as they did at that moment. My mind raced to figure out if there was time to remove my boots, yank off my socks, offer them to the man and pull both boots back on before the subway reached my destination. I had scarcely completed this thought when the conductor hit the brakes.

Feeling a strange desperation to offer something to a man who had asked for nothing, I reached into my coat pocket and retrieved its contents: two dollars. *It's not enough*, I thought. But the train had come to a halt, so I got up hastily, pushed the bills deep into one of the man's bags and, apparently unnoticed by him, scooted off the train just as its doors were closing. In the days that followed, I occasionally thought about the man, wondered about the face behind all that hair, and imagined him shuffling through his bag and happening upon the money. Would he see it as a small token of compassion, or as no more than a means of returning to the subway for couple of more nights?

When, whether, and what to give are questions everyone in New York has to contend with, no matter where in that city of contrasts one abides. I know one fellow who tore the want ads out of the newspaper each morning and folded them into his breast pocket. Sometimes, when approached for handouts on his way to or from work, he would invite the solicitor to a café and offer to help them hunt the ads for work. Nearly everyone rejected his offer, but occasionally someone accepted. Once, someone even got a job. But this fellow is rare. Most of us pass by extended hands like priests and Levites on the road to Jericho.

One builds up defenses in a big city and develops self-survival blinders that are not easily penetrated. The needs of people can be so desperate, so constant, that one closes her eyes because she imagines that to open them is to be overwhelmed or irrevocably obligated—or both. One day, while walking down Second Avenue in my old neighborhood, I saw ahead of me a stream of people detouring around something on the sidewalk. When I reached the detour I discovered they were all avoiding a body sprawled on the pavement. I, too, walked around the figure. For the next two blocks and all the way up my apartment steps, I thought about that man. I took off my coat and hung it up, chiding myself with the question, *How much effort would it have taken to hoist the fellow up and sit with him at the corner café over a warm drink?* Then I sat down on the couch and tried to read. It was useless.

I put my coat back on, ran down the steps and hurried to the place where I'd passed the man. But he was gone. Had he pulled himself up?  Had someone with more courage and heart than I happened by?  My friend with his want ads?

Two weeks after encountering the man who'd been sleeping on the train, I again turned into an Upper West Side subway entrance to ride the Red Line on its late night run. Glancing down the stairwell, I spotted a figure crowned with a mass of woolly black hair.  He wore a cumbersome gray-blue coat, held together with a belt of rags.  I called *hello* to that familiar coat, and the man inside it looked up, revealing his face.  The face, as much as the coat, seemed familiar. I saw in it all the ups and downs of the human experience.

Without thinking, I bounded down the steps as if an old friend waited for me at the bottom.  I walked up to the man and heard myself ask, "Do you need money for the train?"  Startled, he responded by opening his palm to show me a handful of pennies and nickels.  "I don't need all of it; I already have 15 cents," he told me.

Responding to the strength, as well as to the struggle of that outstretched hand, I gave him the rest of the fare. Then he, with that face I somehow knew, gave me a crescent moon smile that made me the debtor.

## MOON OVER MANHATTAN

*Why not become the one who lives with a full moon in each eye?* ~Hafiz

Not even the showy lights of New York City can outdo the moon on nights when she presents her face. I have vivid childhood memories of seeing her shining over the East River from the expansive living room windows in my grandparents' Manhattan apartment. They lived on the fifth floor of Beekman Terrace, a charming, six-story brick building constructed in 1924 at the very end of East 51st Street. Their huge living-dining room featured high ceilings and spanned nearly forty feet, with tall, broad windows flanking the east and south walls. Looking eastward, we saw the southern tip of Franklin D. Roosevelt Island and beyond that Queens. To the northeast, we could see the Queensboro Bridge just upriver. And gazing downriver, we had a distant view of Williamsburg Bridge—the "other" suspension bridge that connects lower Manhattan to Brooklyn. Plying up and down the river were chunky red tugboats that looked straight out of a fairy tale to my child eyes. All of these river markers were lit at night, making the water sparkle. When the moon joined the scene, she was first violin in a symphony of light.

In my growing up years, visiting my grandparents in Manhattan gave thrilling contrast to my regular life in Michigan. My sister and I lived with our parents in a ranch-style home planted in the former cornfield of a farmland-turned-suburbia neighborhood. There, when not in school, we spent our days biking on dirt roads, hunting for reptiles along a woodland stream, swimming or ice skating at the nearby lake, and playing flashlight tag on moonless nights. New York presented a totally different playground—not just performances at Radio City and the Met or dinosaurs at the Natural History Museum, but subways, escalators, elevators, and endless concrete sidewalks where we could roller skate to our hearts' content. Our skates were stored in our grandparents' front hall closet. They were the old-fashioned kind: steel wheels attached to a metal foot plate, with a key used to adjust length and width. Upon arrival, as soon as allowed, we'd retrieve them and run down to the neighborhood park, which stretched southward along the river and offered two full blocks of hard walkways.

I can't recall a single time when I was anything less than excited about going to New York to visit these grandparents. But as time passed, the reasons for my enthusiasm changed. As an adult, I was drawn not so much by the city as by them, by their fascination with life. When traveling out of the country for work, I almost always routed myself through Manhattan so I could see them. I relished their celebratory send-offs and their keen interest in hearing the long version of my travel stories when I returned. They had made dozens of their own trips to many parts of the world, my grandmother hauling her painting equipment, my grandfather squeezing books into the luggage. They explored together, and when they came upon a scene she wanted to paint, she'd set up her easel and he'd settle in close by to read while she worked. They took great pleasure in one another's company, and seeing them together never failed to remind me that good marriages are possible. That was another reason I loved going to see them.

During one visit when I was twenty-something and they were in their 80s, we lingered at the dining table after one of my grandmother's colorful international meals. Although it was just the three of us, two candelabras lit the table. Eating by candlelight was customary in their home. She liked the romance of it and the fact that soft lighting made it possible to see the night scene through the big window alongside the table. That night we could see city lights dotting the silhouettes of buildings and trees. The river glistened with a sweep of moonshine and a pointillist parade of reflected light from the boats and barges gliding along its back. It was an artful backdrop for my grandmother's lively stories. She was a deft storyteller, able to turn anything—person, pet, or incident—into an irresistible tale.

That night, as usual, her narrative held me in rapt attention. At one point, however, I happened to glance over at my grandfather and something in his gaze caught my eye and held it for a moment. Looking back at her and then again at him, I realized what it was: He and I were not seeing the same person. His expression told it all. While I was hearing a story, he was beholding layers of being in the woman he'd loved for a lifetime.

They had grown up next door to each other in Brooklyn, and she had fascinated him from the time they were young kids sneaking into his father's bakery to help themselves from the huge raisin crock. At first, she fancied his older brother and my grandfather was just the little guy they sent on errands. But, as the years passed, he was the one who finally won her full heart. She delighted in his attentiveness and valued his distinctly poetic yet practical nature. He admired her artistry—the wild hats she made (and wore!) and especially the serious way she pursued painting. One summer, as a teenager, she traveled by train to Woodstock, located a boarding house, and worked her way into the famous artists' colony there. She returned year after year. Eventually, after she married my grandfather and he became a successful lawyer, they bought a stone cottage in

Woodstock and she spent summers there with their daughters.

During those warm months, my grandmother devoted many hours to painting every day. She continued taking classes with several of the illustrious painters who also summered there, and took great pride when her work hung alongside theirs in regional exhibitions. Her daughters spent their days practicing long hours at the piano, having lessons with their piano teacher, and participating in the Woodstock Youth Orchestra—when not posing for her or helping her tend a sprawling vegetable garden. Unfailingly, my grandfather came for the weekends, which featured garden parties, a library fair, chamber music in a woodland concert hall, and the annual Maverick Festival. For the festival, rich with music and theatrical performances, revelers donned costumes and pranced about as if they lived in Shakespeare's *A Midsummer Night's Dream.*

Without my grandmother, it is likely that my grandfather would have passed all his days tied up in tax and estate law and all his evenings living vicariously through the classical literature he loved. With her, he was engulfed in real life creativity and adventure.

So, what did he see as we listened to her tell a story by a big picture window in their twilight years? Clearly, he perceived far more in her eyes than antique blue in twin beds of wrinkles. Looking through layers of time, he could see the taut translucent skin that once surrounded a young girl's wondering, bright-eyed vision. He could recall keen focused eyes confident in communicating form and color to hands skilled in painting. He could detect the demanding, love-filled eyes of a mother directing their children. The solemnity of mature eyes aware that naïve and easy perception has departed. The flash of fading eyes indignant when they faltered. Eyes that, year after year, reserved a particular look for him alone.

Watching my grandfather watch my grandmother, I knew he was seeing so much more in her than I had begun to imagine. He looked at her with full-moon eyes. That's the beauty of long-knowing: If we let it inform us, it provides a more complete and therefore more accurate view, perhaps not only of an individual, but of life itself. My grandfather did not see my grandmother narrowly as an old woman. He saw her as all ages, and thereby ageless. He saw her as herself. Realizing this made me look at her—and him—with new eyes. It taught me to look for the layers in everyone I meet.

For me, on that moonlit night in Manhattan, this was the best show in town.

## PSALM OF LIFE

*When on my bed the moonlight falls.* . . .
~Alfred, Lord Tennyson

My grandfather spent more than sixty years with the same woman, and after her passing he continued to enrich his life. He was 87 when she died, yet he earnestly continued to go to work every day—not because there was much to do at his old Brooklyn law office, but because she had always told him retirement was a foolish way to spend one's days. This "up and doing" approach to life was a lasting gift she had given him.

Another reason he went to work, I believe, was that he loved coming home at the end of the day, opening the door to their apartment, and calling, "Darling, I'm home!" I don't think he imagined for a moment that she would reappear to take his hat and kiss him a welcome. It was simply that some things were not as they seemed. Despite her absence, she was always there, held in his heart inextricably, like a new moon just out of sight.

One of the last times I talked with her, she confided that after all their years together, her heart still "leaped" each day when she heard him open the door after his day at the office. Since she was an artist, one might assume that her creative imagination conjured up such romantic impulses, but I doubt that, for I saw them greet each other time and time again, and always—remarkably—there was freshness in their daily reunions. Room for surprise and change, mixed with a love of the familiar. This was a gift they gave each other.

After she left, he began sleeping in her bed, an arm's reach from his own. Whenever one of his children or grandchildren came to visit, he invited them to sleep in his old bed rather than in the guest room, because he enjoyed talking deep into the night. I visited quite often, and discovered that he spent much of his work day at the law office napping on a couch, which meant that he rarely felt like sleeping through an entire night. At 1 a.m. he would flip on the lamp by his bed and begin chatting. When he'd had enough, he would switch off the light, often mid-sentence, and doze. But at 3:15, it was on with the light and conversation once again.

The first time this happened, I chided him for keeping me awake. But gradually, I grew accustomed to the fact that he took increasingly little notice of time. He developed a schedule of his own which, at home and office alike, consisted of working, napping, eating, and talking exactly when he felt like it. This was life in the present tense.

It tired me out, yet there was a serendipity to it that charmed me.

One night in the summer of 1985, he never turned off the light at all. He just talked, reminisced, and recited poems. He had a passion for poetry and literature. In all of his many books he had penciled on the fly leaves the dates when he read them. Some, like Tolstoy's *Anna Karenina*, had two or three dates noted. He delighted in telling of his eccentric literature professors at Columbia University, particularly one aristocratic fellow who always wore a flamboyant black cape: "He would arrive in a big black limousine with a chauffeur and a footman! We would all rush to the window to watch the footman drop a little set of steps by the car door and help the old gentleman out."

So my grandfather was in his element reciting poems that night when the light stayed on. They were old classic verses whose memorization had been the stuff of his education. More than one mentioned the moon, including Emily Bronte's "Moonlight, Summer Moonlight":

'Tis moonlight, summer moonlight
All soft and still and fair;
The solemn hour of midnight
Breathes sweet thoughts everywhere. . . .

As the night wore on, he mulled over Shakespeare's sonnets. He whispered the poems that Robert and Elizabeth Browning wrote for one another. At one point, he started a poem I didn't recognize, only to stop after the first two lines: "Tell me not, in mournful numbers/Life is but an empty dream . . ."

"What is that?" I asked.

He thought for a moment. Then, unable to remember the title, the poet, or the rest of the poem, he moved on to Keats and Donne. But several times, he returned to that unknown poem, saying its opening lines slowly, thoughtfully: "Tell me not . . ." It sounded terribly sad to me. I told him so. "Yes, it does appear so, doesn't it?" he said. "But it's not, really."

The next day I left on a writing assignment that took me away for six weeks. I was on my way home by way of New York City and, as always, made a stop at my grandparents' apartment. But my grandfather was gone— forever.

Once back to my own home, the partial poem he had recited during our last night haunted me: "Tell me not in mournful numbers/Life is but an empty dream." I found myself repeating the words again and again. They still seemed sad to me, even ominous. Were they a verbal threshold leading to a dark commentary about death and about life's futility? At the end of his years did my grandfather have deep regrets he never told me of, but hinted at with this poem? Was this man, who had lived with such a positive attitude, retracting his life example and giving me a warning? I pulled out my poetry books and looked for the lines. I could not find them.

A few months later, over breakfast, I told this story to a friend who teaches poetry and literature. To my surprise, he told me that the lines came from a well-known poem by the famous Longfellow.

After breakfast, I went straight to the library and found a collection of the poet's work. It happened to be a well-worn, turn-of-the-century edition, one I could easily imagine my grandfather poring over.

As I read, my dreary questions ended and I discovered what my grandfather meant when he told me, "Yes, it does appear sad, but it's not really." For the poem is entitled, "A Psalm of Life." In its entirety, it is about life's great purpose that survives all time and transitions. It is about the lasting gifts we give one another, and about leaving footprints for each other to help us find the way.

### A Psalm of Life

Tell me not, in mournful numbers,
Life is but an empty dream! —

For the soul is dead that slumbers,
And things are not what they seem.

Life is real! Life is earnest!
And the grave is not its goal;
Dust thou art, to dust returnest,
Was not spoken of the soul.

Not enjoyment, and not sorrow,
Is our destined end or way;
But to act, that each tomorrow
Find us farther than today.

Art is long, and Time is fleeting,
And our hearts, though stout and brave,
Still, like muffled drums, are beating
Funeral marches to the grave.

In the world's broad field of battle,
In the bivouac of Life,
Be not like dumb, driven cattle!
Be a hero in the strife!

Trust no Future, howe'er pleasant!
Let the dead Past bury its dead!
Act,– act in the living Present!
Heart within, and God o'erhead!

Lives of great men all remind us
We can make our lives sublime,
And, departing, leave behind us
Footprints on the sands of time;

Footprints, that perhaps another,
Sailing o'er life's solemn main,
A forlorn and shipwrecked brother,
Seeing, shall take heart again.

Let us, then, be up and doing,
   With a heart for any fate;
  Still achieving, still pursuing,
  Learn to labor and to wait.
           *Henry Wadsworth Longfellow*

Bunny McBride

## THE PROPOSAL

*The new moon begins a new chapter of our nights.*
~Rainer Maria Rilke

My husband asked me to marry him three times, but I lacked the courage to say yes. Although I loved him dearly, I hesitated because my first marriage had come to a sad conclusion, and I couldn't bear the possibility of another relationship falling short of its lifetime promise. Remarkably, he didn't give up on me. However, he said he would never ask me again. If we were going to wed, the invitation would have to come from me. He had only one request: "Ask me in a memorable place."

On an early spring day nearly a year later, he stopped by my writing studio in the afternoon as he often did. This time he had come for a specific reason—to tell me that his father had phoned from the Netherlands. Fond of his dad, I lit up and said something like, "So how's he doing? What's new?"

"Well, he reminded me that when you first met him and my mother at their home five years ago, they loved you and welcomed you as a daughter. And now he wants to know when you will actually become that. In short, he asked when we're getting married."

"What did you tell him?"

"The truth. I said I didn't know and that he'd have to ask you."

"Oh."

"So he asked me to have you call him back."

"What?"

"He wants you to phone him and let him know what's up."

"That's not really his question to ask," I said, feeling slightly miffed.

"I know, but it's only because he's so fond of you."

I put on my boots and took my coat off a hook by the door.

"What are you doing?" he asked.

"I don't have a phone here, so I'm going back home with you to call your father."

I may have slammed the door when we stepped outside for the short walk. Halfway there, he said, "So, what are you going to tell him?"

"That we're getting married pretty soon." I sounded a bit exasperated when I said this.

"That's news to me," he laughed. Then he added, "My father did call and he told me to give you his love—but I made up the part about him asking you to call him back to say when we're going to marry."

My mouth flew open in dumbfounded surprise. I jumped in the air. I punched him in the shoulder. Finding my voice, I yelled, "You've got to be kidding!" and a bunch of other words. He chuckled. Then I started laughing and I couldn't stop. To my own surprise, I was ready to get married—ready to act out of love rather than fear.

But first, I needed to propose, and that required a special setting. Every plan I made fell through. Then, in June, we both had some work in Washington, DC, near where my parents lived. Anticipating our visit, Mom called to ask if we'd like to hear a National Symphony Orchestra outdoor concert at Wolf Trap. "Yes!" I said, asking if she could get tickets on the lawn rather than covered seating. I was picturing a moonlit summer night and me whispering, "Will you marry me?" during the lyrical 3rd movement of Beethoven's 9th Symphony. After that, I imagined us telling my parents about our plans during "Ode to Joy" in the 4th movement.

The night came, clear and balmy. The moon shone. We parked the car, walked to the entrance, past the ticket taker and onto the lawn. We found a perfect spot with a slight incline and spread out our two blankets. Then, just as we were settling in, my dad leaned over and said, "Honey, I'm so sorry, but I'm not feeling well. Would you mind going with me to find a place where we can sit closer to the toilets? Harald can stay here at this better spot with Mom since he's never been to Wolf Trap before. I'm really sorry, but it will be special for your mother to sit with him."

Under the moon on a blanket with my father next to the toilets on my engagement night? Unbelievable.

The next day, with no proposal to celebrate, the two of us left for New York City. We planned to spend a couple of days there before I flew to the Arctic Circle for a magazine assignment. While in the city, I overnighted with my grandfather. Harald stayed with an old friend, but he accompanied me to my grandfather's place to say hello. They had great affection for one another. Close to his 90th birthday, my grandfather had been under the weather for a few weeks and was propped up in bed when we arrived. After visiting for a while, Harald pulled me aside and said, "He doesn't look well. You're going to be gone for six weeks, so before you leave you might want to let him know if you have any plans for us." My heart sank as I realized what he was saying. We returned to my grandfather's bedroom together.

I told him, "I have some news for you."

"Yes?"

"We're going to be married."

"Wonderful!" His face came alive. "When?"

"Well, that's the problem. After Harald proposed to me and I wasn't ready to say yes, he said I would have to do the asking. I'm ready now, but he made me promise to do that in a memorable place, and every time I've planned something, it hasn't worked out."

"What's wrong with right here?" my grandfather asked.

So it happened. Going forward with love rather than being held back by fear, I reached for one of Harald's hands and each of us took one of my grandfather's. And in that little circle, I proposed.

He paused before answering, "Well, I'm not sure." Then he grinned and said yes. Beaming, my grandfather insisted on calling my parents right away. I dialed the number and handed him the phone. "The kids are here," he announced, "and I've just presided over the nuptials!"

After spending two days with my grandfather, I kissed him goodbye and left for the airport. It was our last kiss— memorable, just like the proposal. He had used the last bit of light in his own life to dispel the shadow of divorce from mine.

Bunny McBride

# PALE WINTER MOON

*We see but what we have the gift of seeing; what we bring we find.*
~Henry Wadsworth Longfellow

In the cold heart of mid-winter, I stepped out of my apartment for a late night walk—a few trips around the block to clear my head and sort through a problem, now forgotten. I lived in Boston's South End, a corner of the Back Bay that I was drawn to because of its richly mixed population with dozens of different ethnic groups. My street, flanked by 4-story brownstones built in the 19th century, was home to several boarding houses and bookended by big subsidized apartments. The neighborhood was undergoing gentrification, but in no great hurry to get there. It had a reputation for crime, and many people felt unsafe walking there at night. Yet, I always felt at ease. I had the advantage of working at a community drop-in center for low-income minority kids—the Boston Forum. It offered tutoring and big brother/sister programs, all kinds of workshops, plus summer day camp. I knew the families in the neighborhood through the kids. I celebrated with them when their older sons got out of jail and joined in their efforts to keep the younger ones from following in those footsteps. I'd learned that there were many layers to those who did time for crime and that their mothers almost always knew how to excavate to the strata that held the heart. I tried to do the same. Occasionally, guys who turned to thievery brought me gifts from questionable sources. Stolen goods delivered with loving intentions put me in a quandary that prompted a curious mix of thanks and frank discussion. But my neighbors also gave me the truest, most meaningful gift: the feeling of being safe, watched over by the community.

So it was that on that late-night, midwinter walk, I felt no trepidation. It was a relief to be outside, as alone with my thoughts as the moon hidden behind the veil of that overcast night. Snow fell lightly, dusting the sidewalk. As I approached the alleyway that ran between my street and the next, I noticed a man I hadn't seen before ambling toward me. We were the only two people in view and we reached the alley at the same moment. I glanced up and said hello. Taking me off guard, he grabbed me by the shoulders and forced me into the alley. Shaken, but not yet afraid, I tried to engage him. I mentioned that I hadn't seen him before, asked his name, where he lived. I figured he must be related to someone I knew, and if I could find out who that was, we'd have a connection and all would be well. When I talked, he stopped pushing. When I stopped talking, he pushed. He said almost nothing—until he pulled out a knife, held it to my throat, and threatened sexual violence in frighteningly graphic language.

He turned me from the main alleyway into the narrow corridor that ran behind the backside of the brownstone houses on my street. As he pressed me along, we got closer to the lamp post that rose up in the darkness. Suddenly, I got a good look at his eyes—dark and distracted—and realized I wasn't getting through to him. Then I was scared. Really scared. I screamed and shoved him with all my might. He reacted by nicking me in the neck with his knife, then letting go and running off. I had been ready to run, so it was so strange to stand there, as the victim, and watch my attacker tear down the alley. Strange, unsettling and somehow terribly sad. Once he was out of sight, I walked to my home, sat on the curb and cried, lamenting the fear—both mine and his. When I went inside, my husband and a friend who lived with us tended to me and called the police.

After being interviewed by an officer and cleaning the bit of blood from my neck, I went to bed. Lying among the shadows in my room, I thought about what had happened. I had been nicked, not cut, which suggested my assailant had at least some reservations about hurting me. Of course, I was grateful to have avoided real harm, but truly troubled that my release had come about through a hard shove and a frantic scream. I had acted out of absolute fear, something I had never felt in my neighborhood before. Working at the community center had given me a strong sense of security, along with a skill set that, until now, had served me well. I had experienced finding common ground, talking people out of trouble, building relationships. But not this time. Clearly, social savvy, ingenuity, or cleverness didn't ensure safety. I felt robbed of my most valued possession—trust.

I contemplated this throughout the following week, searching for some missing element in the way I'd handled the situation. And then it came to me: I was not the creator of relationships. Rather, some intrinsic relationship must exist between every two people—a graceful fitting of their inner cores of goodness waiting to be discerned and then realized. With some, that core and fit are easily recognized; with others, they are well hidden and may require keen insight and considerable patience and courage to find. But I had the inkling that starting with this premise would change the way I saw, treated, and responded to people—all creatures, actually. If true, it could open hearts. It could quell fear, fuel intuition, guide communication, invite adjustments, and breed trust. It would make us feel safe *with* each other, not *from* each other. I could not impose the premise on anyone, but living from it presented possibilities that fear and defensiveness inevitably shroud. I didn't know it at the time, but these thoughts were preparation for something just around the corner.

A dozen days after that incident, I stood in my kitchen around midnight, pouring steaming cocoa into mugs for my sister and me, savoring the sweet chocolaty aroma. With a cup in each hand, I returned to the living room, pausing to switch on the outside light that illuminated the small courtyard behind my ground floor apartment. To my delight, I saw that after a long day of steady snowfall, the skies had cleared. I joined my sister on the couch where we'd been curled up for hours talking. Sitting sideways on opposite ends, with our legs and feet under a shared cover, we marveled at the avalanche of snow beyond the living room window. No longer falling from the sky, it had settled over the scene, thickening the tree branches, heightening the fence, blanketing the patio. Curiously, the snow appeared more warm than cold. It looked so serene and inviting that we couldn't resist going outside.

The city was astoundingly still: empty streets below a clear night sky holding ice chip stars and a pale half-moon. The frosty air smelled pure and bright, as if it had never before been breathed by anyone. Clad in high boots and a huge hooded down parka that hung to my knees, every inch of me was warm, except for my face, which felt washed and alive in that cold fresh air.

Tramping along unshoveled sidewalks, we made our way to a nearby park. Entering the gate, my sister took the lead and we toddled single file through the foot-high snow on a narrow path made by several earlier pioneers. If ever there was a peaceful walk through the city, this was it.

All at once, without warning, two strong arms encircled me from behind. Startled, I gasped, "Oh!" My sister wheeled around. About 10 feet ahead, she started toward me and the stranger holding me in his grip. But then, reconsidering, she turned and ran off in the other direction to find help.

Tightening his hold, my assailant snarled, "Give me your wallet!"

Speaking quickly, I told him the truth: "I have no wallet. We're just out walking because it's such a beautiful night with all this snow."

I think that only then, hearing my voice, did he realize I was a woman. Yanking down the hood of my parka, he spun me around, bringing us face to face. "Then give me a kiss," he demanded, bringing his lips down on mine with so much force that our teeth knocked. We fell into the deep snow. His face smothered mine as he held me down. Then, in an instant, something caught my attention: His only protection against the cold was a thin windbreaker and he was shaking uncontrollably. I thought I felt his heart beating, but it may have been my own. At that moment, it flashed through my mind that this event was not about someone trying to steal my money or harm me. It was a cry for help.

That insight, merged with the realizations that had come while contemplating the previous assault, gave me courage. I felt, beyond doubt, that this man and I were already connected in some deep way. My conviction not only quelled fear, but also stirred intuition and guided communication. I didn't try to talk him out of anything or figure out who we might know in common. Instead, I heard myself say, "What are you really looking for?"

No response, except a slight loosening of his hold.

My heart opened a bit more: "Are you okay?"

A long pause, followed by, "No, I'm not."

"Can you tell me why?" I asked, as he let go and helped me up.

And so our brief conversation began. He was alone, homeless. He had been on his way to the Pine Street Shelter when he saw my sister and me and decided to take a detour in our direction. I told him about the community center where I worked and said he was welcome to stop by there. By the time I saw my sister hurrying in our direction with the man she'd asked for help, I was walking arm in arm with the man who had jumped me. "That's my sister coming," I said. "We're going home now." He apologized and said, "Thank you." I shook his hand and then kissed him on the cheek—"like a sister," he proclaimed.

We'd found our graceful fitting. Parting ways, we promised each other a more peaceful greeting next time. Meanwhile, the pale half-moon still hung in the sky overhead, its soft light trailing after each one of us as he found his way to the shelter and my sister and I returned home.

## A THIN PLACE

*The moon rises, so beautiful it . . .*
*makes me take measure of myself:*
*one iota, pondering heaven.*

~Mary Oliver

When my husband and I moved to Kansas, our East Coast friends gave us their condolences. Some actually sent sympathy cards with messages like, "Our hearts go out to you in this time of sorrow" and "May your memories give you strength." Everyone we told responded, *"Kan-*sas?!*"*, emphasizing the first syllable in a way that grimaced their mouths. None of them had ever been there, but that did not curb their negative comments, all delivered with a mix of amazement, sarcasm, and pity. I couldn't count the number of Dorothy, Toto, and Yellow Brick Road jokes that came our way. However, to my amusement, they fell flat with my Dutch husband who has never seen "The Wizard of Oz." For him, Kansas was the romantically rustic land of Dodge City, cowboys, and Indians. When people said, "Wow, you're moving to the middle of nowhere," he answered, straight faced, "Well no, just look at a map of the U.S. Kansas is right in the middle, halfway to everywhere."

We were going because he had accepted a professorship there. What could I do? He had moved to the States for me a decade earlier, and now it was my turn to relocate for him.

After weeks of disparaging comments about our impending move, I had become almost apologetic about it. So I was a bit thrown off when a poetry professor friend responded to the news with obvious pleasure, "Oh, Kansas! Where in Kansas?"

"In the Flint Hills," I sputtered.

"You know, when I drove through those hills, I found them so beautiful that I had to stop and write a poem."

I was so grateful, I kissed him.

Two months before our move, I flew to Kansas to look for a house. The university had offered just one plane ticket for the search, so my spouse graciously gave it to me, knowing what a nester I am and trusting the fact that we have very similar taste. He made just one request: "Try to find a place in the hills near the lake and some woods." This, of course, did not match my imagined sense of the state, but he assured me that it was there for the finding. He knew, because the head of the department had taken him on a drive to his home, situated in just such a setting, twenty minutes from the university.

So I made my first trip to Kansas with that in mind. As I descended the steps of the 16-seater plane onto the runway, I saw a building that reminded me of remote airports I'd used in Africa. Above the single entrance was a sign: "Manhattan, the Little Apple." At least they have a sense of humor, I thought.

Within two days, I found a home in the kind of surroundings my husband had described, just five miles north of campus: a wooden house nestled into a hill on four acres of land at the edge of an oak and cedar forest, with a view on a lake backed by undeveloped rolling hills. We had neighbors, but nature screened their houses from view. And there were still hundreds of acres of nearby ranchland on our side of the lake. This was suburbia in disguise. At the time, I didn't know that the home I chose was on a major bird migration route that would gift us with seasonal visits by tens of thousands of birds—snow geese, Canadian geese, white pelicans, and others.

Despite this idyllic setting, I never imagined Kansas would be a muse or a place for epiphanies. But, for two decades now, it has been that, many times over. I've always found solace in walking and that has been especially true in the Flint Hills. I hike them for sheer pleasure or when I have a problem that needs solving, be it an impasse in writing, an emotional or health challenge, a relational conflict. For me, there are few things in life that can't be improved by ambling across a piece of earth.

One late autumn afternoon I took to the hills after an argument with my husband. It was one of those "about nothing" altercations, fueled by defensiveness, self-justification, poor listening, and personal egos. The idea of ego had been on my mind for several months, ever since attending a seminar on the topic. "Wouldn't it be wonderful," asked the speaker, "to have someone say to you a year from now, 'What's going on with you? You seem so open, serene, and imperturbable.'? That's what happens when you surrender personal ego, when you turn your vantage point from the self and act on behalf of something more inclusive, when you see yourself as an expression of the One Divine Ego." His point, as I understood it, was not to wipe out one's identity, but rather to get to the heart of the true, essential self which is intricately connected to every other expression of life. He was calling for a shift in how we thought about identity, inviting us to see what would happen if we lived from the standpoint that we and every other creature are distinct but inseparable emanations of Life itself—of the Great I AM, the One Ego, God, Divine Mind, the Force, Love with a capital L, whatever one chooses to call Universal

Being. This idea appealed to me. It made sense to me. I'd been trying to do it. But, clearly, I'd lost track of it in that silly but troublesome marital clash. At that moment, I felt quite separate from the Universal Being and from my husband.

I thought about this as I marched my way to the old dirt track that climbs the gentle slope to southern end of my favorite ridge. From there, one can take a long walk that offers views of hills in every direction and of the lake sprawled along the east side valley just below. Upon reaching the hilltop, I slowed my pace and vowed not to come down until I gained some new insight about ego that would transform or at least improve communication. I had faith that would happen because I had already experienced the Flint Hills as a "Thin Place"—an area where, according to ancient Celtic belief, the distance between heaven and earth collapses and we catch glimpses of the divine.

I walked and walked, gradually letting go of my inner grumbling. But by the time I reached the north end of the ridge, no epiphany had come. I sat down. I waited. I wondered if I would have to spend the night. Settling into patience, I drank in the scene—its grassy smell, its tawny colors, and a breeze that presented itself in sound, motion, and touch. These hills of limestone and flint are old and humble, worked and reworked by nature's hand. Once wrapped in shallow seas, they were worn down by water and weather. Unlike the Rocky Mountain range with its showy individual peaks, the Flint Hills fold into each other so that it is often hard to tell where one ends and the next begins. They seem to be holding each other up. Capped with clayey soil full of flinty gravel, they are more suited to ranching than farming. So they have not been destroyed by plows and are still covered with native grasses—big bluestem, switch grass, Indian grass—one of the last great preserves of tallgrass prairie in the country.

Sitting at the end of the ridge, facing north, I was enveloped in the collective embrace of that hill's rounded companions, rolling out to the horizon in every direction. To the west, the sun announced the day's end in a bold symphony of color as it slid behind the hills there. Simultaneously, a full moon rose quietly in the east above the hills flanking the lake. Unable to keep my eyes on the sun's hard glare, I gave my attention to the softer, reflected light of the moon. It was huge, orange, and draped a shimmering path across the gray-blue water.

I sat there a long time watching the moon rise in the darkening sky. It looked so open. The way I wanted to be. Noticing the soft breeze lifting my hair ever so slightly, I closed my eyes, all the better to feel it. And then came an idea in the form of a poem. It arrived in one piece, and while it's not great poetry, it spoke to me:

High on a hill
I surrendered my will
and found I was still
within
One Kingdom
Come!
ego be done –
taken away on the wind.

To me, at that moment, the wind was *spiritus*, God's breath, and it occurred to me that *this* is what sweeps away personal ego and its many pitfalls. But for that to happen, I'd have to open myself up as a passageway and allow that breath to do its work. I'd have to set aside personal ego with its determination to be right, to justify itself, to win, to impose guilt, or to hold on to something out of pride. I'd have to make space for God's grace, for Divine Love to breathe through me and express the true emanation I was created to be. It was such a simple idea, and in a way I already knew it. But now I *felt* it working on me and in me. It felt good. And its arrival meant that I didn't have to spend the night on the ridge after all.

I got up and began making my way back along the hillcrest. Feeling celebratory, I sang to myself, choosing an old hymn that begins "I walk with Love along the way, and oh it is a holy day." Coming to the second stanza—"Who walks with Love along the way shall *talk with Love* and Love obey"—I stopped in my tracks. Here was a second part to the epiphany, something beyond surrendering my personal ego to the One Divine Ego: In my daily encounters I could choose to "talk with Love,"—to reach beyond the personal egos of others and speak to their God-given natures, their true inner selves. And as they spoke, I could open my heart and mind more fully, aiming to discern and respond to the point behind their words or tone—to their deep desires and thoughts. This may sound strange, but I actually had an image of reaching into my husband's mouth, pulling out a golden strand of meaning, and watching everything else in the communication disappear, swept away by *spiritus*.

Now I was done, and ready to return home. The full round moon accompanied me with her reflected light—a quiet reminder to be open and to continually give myself over to being a reflection of the One Divine Ego.

And so it happened in the Flint Hills of Kansas, halfway to everywhere, including heaven.

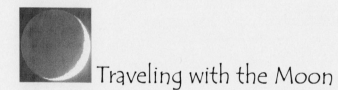Traveling with the Moon

Bunny McBride

## TRAVELING LIGHT

*To enjoy life's immensity, you do not need many things.*

~ Ryokan

In the 1970s, just out of university, I joined the throng of young Americans venturing abroad on the cheap. I planned my journey around three things I longed to see: Goya's paintings at the Prado Museum in Madrid, the ancient city of Carthage in the North African country of Tunisia, and the Holy Lands in Israel. I also wanted to see a boyfriend in Oxford, so England was on the program. Everything between these landmarks was on a list of possibilities. I was 21 at the time, and as my departure date approached, my father asked many times, "Honey, wouldn't you like to take a tour rather than travel all by yourself?" My answer was always the same: No tour matched my special itinerary.

With a modest pack of traveler's checks (purchased with tips saved up from countless hours of waitressing) and a roundtrip plane ticket to London (paid for with college graduation gifts), I began my open ended journey. I figured it would last until my resources ran out. That turned out to be four months, thanks to hitchhiking and the many generous and enterprising souls I encountered along the way.

In Tunis, capital city of Tunisia, I met a fellow named Paul who was writing a hitchhiker's guide to the Mediterranean. Our plans overlapped somewhat, so we traveled together for a couple of weeks. He carried only a wooden flute (which he played beautifully enough to win many a gratis meal) and a small rucksack. I, too, had a rucksack, albeit twice as large as his. I also had a purse the size of a prize-winning pumpkin, plus a small piece of retro luggage known as a train case—a hard-shelled rectangular box with a grip handle on the top. The case was as cumbersome as it was heavy, and grew more so with each mile of our journey, which included hours of walking as well as riding.

While in Tunis, Paul and I stayed in our respective low-end pensions, taking day trips together to Carthage and little fishing villages along the coast. It was only when we met at the port to hop a boat to the Italian island of Sicily that he saw my luggage. He raised an eyebrow, but didn't say anything other than, "Do you need help carrying all that stuff?"

Getting off the boat at Palermo on Sicily's north coast, we hitched a ride 70 km east to the centuries-old town of Cefalù, nestled against a towering promontory that presses into the Tyrrhenian Sea. I hear Cefalù is a bustling tourist spot today, despite its small size, but during our brief stay it felt intimate and under visited. Happening upon a sweet café overlooking the beach and the long arm of the stone seawall not far beyond, we decided to have dinner there before finding a place to stay for the night. We heaped my luggage on and under a spare chair. It looked like an overweight date to Paul's petite rucksack, slung over the back of his seat.

As we sat there, twilight came, and with it a lovely moon. "Beach walk night," said Paul. And after dinner, that's what we did—with my bags in tow. Midway along the arc of the small beach, we sat on a low wall and watched the waves roll in and out. Paul pulled out his flute and began to play, accompanied by the percussion sounds of the sea. Just when I was thinking that I couldn't be more content, he paused, turned to me and asked, "Did you know that the moon is more beautiful without luggage?"

Despite his gracious hint to pare down, I held on to the whole kit and caboodle, including the train case. This was well before the era of I-Pad, Kindle, and smart phones, and that case contained a precious collection of bulky items: guidebooks, my journal, spiritual literature, a volume of poetry, a novel. In addition—I can't believe I'm admitting this—it held hair curlers, just in case. Dragging my gear around month after month, I took the painful approach to learning the value of the veteran traveler's credo, *travel light*.

Since then, taking up professional writing which kept me on the move, I've sworn by this tenet. For many years now, no matter where I'm going or for how long, I've carried only a small duffle or a carry-on sized roller bag. Pared down to essentials, I can move about unencumbered, light of foot and heart.

But being on the road is not the same as being at home, where, again and again, I find possessions piling up around me. Overwhelmed by them, I clear out closets and cabinets. I take loads to the Salvation Army and the Baptist church resale shop. "Where did all this stuff come from!?" I ask the air, as if I had nothing to do with the accumulation. But of course, I am my own culprit, aided and abetted by a society that refers to its people as "consumers" and defines progress as "technological and material advancement." I know there is much more to us and to life than this. When I stop to think about these soul-stifling definitions, I'm appalled; when I don't stop to think about them, I find myself literally buying into them. Clearly, unless consciously carving a spiritual path through the coercive arena of materialism, it closes in on us.

How to carve that path? I've taken heart and cues from people in far off places who live so lightly that being with them has offered a kind of holy focus. I'll never forget the first time I saw a Maasai tribesman striding across the rolling grasslands of northern Tanzania. I was barreling along in a

Landrover with a photographer and a biologist—and suddenly, there he was in the distance. Built like a willow, he moved across the landscape with long graceful strides. He wore sandals, a throw of red cloth, and a sheathed dagger slipped through the belt that held his dress in place. He carried only a spear and a gourd container for milk or water. It was a humbling experience to watch him disappear over a slope of land, knowing he had miles to go before reaching his mud hut with its barely furnished interior. Such moments, such people, have remained in my mind's eye long after they've passed, giving me needed pause and perspective.

I'm not talking romantic asceticism here. Nor am I being sentimental about the often involuntary material austerity that so many people around the world struggle against. What I'm talking about is balance. About the effect such spare lives have had on me. About the gradual embering down of my own material wants and needs in the face of these lives. About some deep pulse of meaning that beats within me when I spend time with people who know how to read the land, who understand their place in it, and move lightly across it. Sometimes, watching nomads who have few possessions and travel vast distances on foot or atop animals rather than in motorized vehicles, I've wondered if that is how all humans were intended to live. A friend tells me true enlightenment means en*light*enment—casting off material possessions and devotions until there's nothing left to hold one down. Then, laughing, he adds, "There's a reason seekers aren't looking for en*heavy*ment!"

I've yet to hit upon what feels like the right balance, but I'm guided by the simple idea that I don't want material growth to eclipse spiritual growth and the natural world. I'm still in a sizable house with too much stuff in the basement. And I continue to get around by car. But, most evenings I hike the rolling Flint Hills of northeast Kansas where I live. Here survives some of the nation's last tall grass prairie, a holy sanctuary of sprawling, uncluttered space. To me, it resembles the Serengeti Plains of Maasai Country, minus the wildebeest and zebras. When I walk these hills, weaving my way through the purple ironweed and yellow nightshade that bloom among the grasses, I marvel at the fact that the original inhabitants of the Great Plains lived here for thousands of years, yet left no trace—no debris, no landfills, no monuments beyond nature itself. They were like wind on the grass. How lightly they traveled. How lightly they lived.

# BEFORE THE RAIN

*Before the rain begins, I always waken,*
*listening to the world hold its breath.* ~Lianne Spidel

It was late, and I lay on my cot in a small round hut nestled against the Great Rift Wall in northern Tanzania. The stone abode was part of a rugged camp where my biologist brother-in-law spent many years doing wildlife research. I went there to escape the capital city of Dar es Salaam where I'd run into one too many snags in the article I'd been researching. The switch from pavement to earth and from human voices to those of nature was a welcome change. I planned to spend one week at the camp, but remained for five.

As I fell in and out of sleep, moonlight danced with acacia trees, creating lacy shadows on the whitewashed wall opposite my window. A lazy wind sifted through the screen, carrying the sounds of the wild on its back. The call of a nearby leopard resounded about the room—one loud hack followed by a series of muted rasps. A lion bellowed, and even though the big cat was probably some two miles away, I felt the vibrations of its momentous roar.

Overhead, scampering tree hyraxes turned the metal roof into a snare drum, while bush babies cried in the darkness, hyenas laughed menacingly, and baboons barked warnings to each other. Even in the pauses between these sounds, it was never wholly still, for crickets rubbed their wings together incessantly, filling the air with a soft, shrill vibrato.

One voice was missing in this midnight chorus, as it had been since my arrival: the whirr of the small waterfall that usually spilled down the Rift Wall into the riverbed that snakes through the landscape below this hut. In that year of drought, there was no cascade and the watercourse was bone dry. Night masked the desolation. But the harsh light of day revealed a parched and brittle place: Trees were skeletons cowering in the sun, and the whole dusty scene showed itself desperate for a drink.

Yet, remarkably (as the night symphony testified), life continued. Thrilled by its stamina and variety, I liked to begin each day watching it stir in the early morning hours as soon as starlight and moonlight began yielding to Africa's blazing sun. Outside my hut stood an enormous boulder nudging against an unusually tall umbrella acacia. Sitting atop the rock beneath that gnarly flat-topped tree, I could look down on the riverbed 100 feet below and witness wondrous sights—such as elephants digging wells.

They arrived at dawn, massive forms lumbering through the veil of incandescent orange that plays over morning scenes there. Reaching the dry riverbed, they began their work, using their forefeet and trunks to quarry subterranean streams. The water table was so low that it took them considerable time, but eventually tiny pools arose and the great beasts quenched their thirst. When the elephants left, other animals arrived to drink from the ephemeral wells— puckish warthogs, playful baboons, graceful impalas and gazelles, and many others.

Day after rainless day, I sat atop my hut-side boulder and watched the scene repeat itself. Then, one morning, something besides the animals caught my attention. At first I didn't see it; I simply *felt* that the setting had somehow changed. Then I looked up and discovered that a green haze had appeared around the crown of the acacia tree—without the benefit of a sprinkle of rain and so very far from the groundwater below. A close look revealed masses of tiny leaf buds.

At breakfast I asked my brother how this happened in the midst of such utter dryness. He told me, "Acacias turn green in anticipation of the rains." He explained that these trees take in water not only with long tap roots but also through their leaves. So, when all is parched, they gear up for growth by sprouting leaves. Then they're able to take maximum advantage of moisture when it finally comes.

"Do you mean," I asked, "that in order to become *really* green, acacias have to muster up a bit of greenness first on their own?"

"Yes. That's it, precisely."

To me, this was a rousing thought. A call to live what one longs for: If you wish to be loved, find a way to give love; if you want knowledge, use whatever bit of wisdom you have to reach out for more; and if you yearn for joy, find a tiny reserve of it and let it trickle from you until it flows. And do so in anticipation. The way an elephant digs for water when it is out of sight. The way an acacia sprouts buds in a full-blown drought.

# SPENDING TIME

*What I want should not be confused with total inactivity.*
*Life is what it is about . . . .* ~ Pablo Neruda

I met D'jibril in the southern Senegalese village of Faoune in West Africa. Warm morning had inched into hot afternoon and I was sitting in a bamboo chair, soaking up the shadows of a silk cotton tree, writing in my journal, and wishing for an orange. Softly, from somewhere, the young boy appeared. He carried a clunky wooden stool under one graceful arm, and a piece of fabric over the other. Between his teeth he held the biggest sewing needle I'd ever seen.

D'jibril placed his stool opposite my chair and sat down. He looked at me with eyes that held all the beginnings that ever were. Before either of us said a word, I was pleased with his company. He greeted me in Fulani and I echoed his *A jaaraama* with a smile. He grinned, and for an instant we were completely bilingual.

Removing the needle from between his teeth—as if grinning had reminded him of its presence—he proceeded to thread it with what looked more like twine than thread. Then, spreading the crumpled fabric across his thighs, he lined up

63

two frayed edges and began to make a seam. The project took all of his concentration—and he won all of mine. I put down my journal, picked up my sketchbook, and began drawing his portrait.

As D'jibril reached the end of the seam, a tiny girl called his name from the doorway of a nearby hut. Except for the beads around her waist, she was naked. I guessed her age to be about three. As soon as D'jibril looked up, she came running. He bit the thread, tied its end in a knot, and held up his handiwork for the child to see. She lifted her arms, and he slid the mended dress over her head. Leaving a giggle in the air, she darted back to the hut. D'jibril's eyes followed her until she disappeared through the entrance of her small mud house. Then he turned to me, obviously delighted, and explained, *"Ma soeur."*

I'd used up my knowledge of Fulani in our greeting, but we found that both of us could speak enough French to communicate. I showed him the portrait I'd started and asked if he'd like to sit back down so I could continue. He did, and we wove easily in and out of conversation as I drew. At one point he slipped away to bring us water from the well. Before returning to his stool, he took a peek at the drawing and smiled broadly. Other than that, he sat very still. Every now and then villagers wandered over to watch me draw for a while, but mostly D'jibril and I had the tree to ourselves. I liked sharing its shade with him. He made me feel as if nothing was more important than sitting there together. As if held in infinity's palm, the two of us whiled away the afternoon, continuing to talk long after the portrait was done.

All at once, I noticed it was dusk. Hard edged shadows had softened. The moon was up and the sun was sliding toward the horizon. Time had passed, unnoticed. Back home, I—like most people there—noticed time a lot. Almost always, it was on our radar. We talked about it and complained about how little of it there was. Searching for ways to save it, people cut corners. Unlike D'jibril and everyone else in his village, we had countless time-saving devices, yet, ironically, we seemed to have less time than they did.

How was it that with an abundance of modern conveniences, we never managed to create a time surplus for leisurely afternoons with one another? In our corner of the world, new wants keep pace with the development of time-saving inventions, and people use each reclaimed minute to produce new things to feed those ever-expanding desires. In the end, we have an excess of things, and spare time remains a phantom. The more we try to save time, the more it seems to become a force that controls our lives and restricts our time together.

D'jibril's community, less conscious of a ticking clock, appeared free from its limitations. It occurred to me that most of them—perhaps all—had never heard the saying, "Time is money." Sitting with D'jibril, I considered the idea that the goal of doing more and more things as quickly as possible to save time may be the biggest waste of time; all too often, it cuts out the very heartbeat of living—true appreciation of what we are doing and of meaningful moments with ourselves and others.

That evening I ate with D'jibril's extended family under the light of the moon supplemented by a kerosene lamp. Dipping our hands into a large shared bowl of rice, vegetables, and spicy peanut sauce, our circle of diners sat or stooped on the ground, faces shimmering in the lamplight. When the bowl was empty, everyone lingered. Cleanup was brief—no dirty dishes beyond the serving bowl and cooking pot—and we were soon settled in for the evening's entertainment of being together.

Now, many years later, I'm sitting on a cushioned chair in my study, wishing for a D'jibril on my footstool. If I close my eyes, I can feel his presence and the lesson he and his community gave me: the lesson of how to *spend* time rather than save it, and the importance of spending it *together*.

## DANCING IN THE DESERT

*Hand in hand, on the edge of the sand,*
*they danced by the light of the moon.* ~Edward Lear

I've never been much of a dancer. Part of the blame belongs to the ballroom dance teachers in the town where I lived my teenage years in the 1960s. After my insufferable first session (white gloves, short boys, and my own writ-large gawkiness as a skinny 5'8" 13-year old), the studio cancelled the class. Years later I learned the reason for that reprieve: The teachers ran off with each other, abandoning their students and spouses.

So, I never learned how to follow a partner's lead—unless you count being waltzed around the living room atop my father's feet as a little girl. I was equally hopeless with the partner-free dances of the day. I didn't nail down that rubber-kneed shuffle called the Mashed Potato until three years after Dee Dee Sharp's record made it famous. By then it was neither "the latest" nor "the greatest." To the tune of my older sister's guffaws, I spent hours trying to master the Bristol Stomp on the linoleum floor in the kitchen. I did it there often, but never dared go public. The Twist, easiest of all dances at the time, was my fallback, but twistin' the night away without doing a single other step was hardly cool. At junior high dances I spent a good deal of time in the bathroom. Most wallflowers retreated to that tiled haven because they feared the humiliation of not being asked to dance. I, however, escaped there because I was panic-stricken that someone might actually ask me.

More recently, in a farming village in the Netherlands, I went to the 25th wedding anniversary celebration of one of the neighbors of my Dutch in-laws. Children, grandparents, people of all ages, were dancing to the merry tunes of violins and accordions. A farmer named Klaas took my hand, hoisted me up onto the dance floor, and began (trying) to twirl me about. For such a big fellow, he was mighty light on his feet. Pathetically, I had no idea what those feet were doing. Every time I moved one of my own feet, I found one of his under it. By the time we finished, I knew he wished he'd left his dancing shoes home and come out in the heavy wooden shoes he wears around his dairy farm.

All of this given, you can imagine that I wasn't into solo performance dancing either. So I wasn't prepared for what happened in the Sahara.

A photographer and I had ventured to the tiny seasonal village of Tin Aicha, Mali, on the southern edge of the Sahara Desert, about 120 kilometers west of Timbuktu. We had gone there to research an article about nomadic Tuareg pastoralists who had survived a severe drought of several years. On our first night in that remote community, we joined our host, Oumarou, for dinner in the courtyard of his humble thatch home. Sitting on the sand with him and several others, we dipped our hands into a large bowl of millet mixed with okra and butter. After we'd eaten our way to the bottom of the bowl, Oumarou brewed strong tea in a small enamel kettle that he propped atop stones in a crackling fire. When the tea became as dark as his sepia eyes, he sweetened it with a great quantity of sugar and poured out a small glass for each of us. He slurped his glass empty and waited for us to do the same. After three rounds of tea, he pulled out his well-worn cassette player. "Now we will dance," he announced, turning on the machine. All at once the haunting whine of the *amzad* (the Tuareg version of a violin) sang from the tape player, transforming the desert's stillness. "Oh no!," I thought, instinctively glancing up toward the heavens for rescue, only to see a crescent moon, poised like bent arms waiting for a dance partner.

Next, without standing up, Oumarou raised his sizeable hands and swirled them high over his head, as if pulling down moonbeams and weaving them into the night breeze. I watched, fascinated. After about fifteen seconds, he lowered his hands and twirled his wrists in slow-motion somersaults.

Then, ever so gracefully, one hand turned away from the other to point at the fellow sitting beside me. At that instant, Oumarou's hands fell to his lap, and my neighbor's rose like a maestro's. Now, long, slender arms swayed and waved like two silk scarves blowing in the wind. Enraptured, I was caught off guard when those arms did a final spiral and the dancer pointed at me. I had no choice but to follow his cue.

Taking a deep breath, I rose to my full sitting height and began dancing with my upper body and arms. My right hand took the lead, and my left followed like a shadow. Something within me came alive. My crossed legs twitched. My toes tapped. I wrote sonnets in the air with my fingertips. I found it difficult to stop. Finally, winding down with a rather dramatic series of sweeping gestures, I pointed to someone else. "How wondrous!" I thought, as he took over the dance. Unlike my artless legs and feet, my arms and hands seemed to possess something verging on expressiveness. Apparently, as far as dancing was concerned, I had been born in the wrong part of the world. I belonged in this place where people dance sitting down. However, I quickly discovered that Tuaregs also dance standing up.

In the middle of our after-dinner dancing, sounds of drumming, chanting, clapping and trilling drifted in our direction, rising in volume until they drowned out the tape cassette. On the other side of the tall, woven grass fence that surrounded Oumarou's home, the women of Tin Aicha had gathered to welcome us. Leading us through an opening in the fence, Oumarou took us to them. They had formed a circle around a fire of gnarled acacia branches. There, under an indigo sky graced by that crescent moon and splashed with stars, one woman after another danced—on her feet—within the circle. To my delight, my photographer friend, and not I, was tapped to perform. Everyone, including me, laughed uproariously as he stirred up the sand with a spirited rendition of the Funky Chicken. I went to bed happy—and relieved.

The following early afternoon, as I sat in my straw hut sketching a young Tuareg woman, I suddenly heard the insistent slapping of a *tamtam* (drum) punctuating the sounds of trilling tongues and clapping hands. "That's curious," I thought—"activity in the high heat of mid-day." Suddenly, two young girls burst into the hut, grabbed me by the hands, and motioned, "Come. Come!" Innocently, I went.

To my chagrin, when I stepped out into the brilliant desert sunlight, I found twenty women waiting to have me dance for them. They had spread out a mat like a stage, and my two escorts ushered me to its center. Then the entire group closed in around that mat, and the vigor of their drumming, clapping and trilling intensified. What could I do? I danced.

As if he were a '60s disc jockey, my photographer friend stood on the sidelines shouting, "Do the Monkey! . . . now the Shingaling! . . . and the Jerk! . . ." I did what he said, and each new dance sent my audience into gales of laughter. After a half dozen numbers, I plopped down on one corner of the mat, feeling exhausted and ridiculous. But for these women, the show had just begun. They kept clapping and trilling and drumming. Some of them were doubled over in laughter. That's how bad I was.

In the middle of their celebratory clamor, it dawned on me. These women didn't care whether I was good or not. They simply wanted what we all want: a good laugh to spice up an ordinary day on the edge of our own particular desert. As their guest, it seemed like the least I could offer. Kissing self-consciousness goodbye, I got up, returned to the center of my wee stage and danced with newly found abandon. The crowd grew, and my friend resumed his calls: "The Swim! . . . the Locomotion! . . . the Twist!"

"What about the Mashed Potato?!" I called. After all, I was prepared for that one.

And so it was that by dancing in the desert, I found a measure of grace—the grace of laughing at myself.

## SALT OF THE EARTH AND STARS

*The moon has become a dancer.* ~Rumi

It has been said that when a stranger sets out into the Sahara, it is like plunging into a sea without knowing how to swim, yet even blind Tuareg nomads have been known to guide caravans across that desert. To them, a dune, a rock, or a few tufts of grass at the feet, or the position of the sun on one's cheek, are infallible signposts. The crooked hands of thorn trees may catch at the stranger, but those who know and see, with or without eyes, move freely in the Bright Country.

For centuries, the Tuareg—tough, haughty, and elegant—maintained the trans-Saharan salt caravan routes from Tunis to Gao, Tlemcen to Timbuktu. Suspended in the middle of austerity, they learned to rely as much on their indomitable spirit as on the sparse gifts of the soil or the meager material goods of the oases. Their world bred in them extremes of stoicism, harshness, resilience. More than that, it taught them to see. For as they struggled to survive within that resonating note of space, they learned to read the subtle signs, the details of life: to identify a person by the mark of a single toe in the sand; to know one's camel from afar by the

73

way it ascends a dune; to recognize a veiled Tuareg by his eyes alone; to locate the scent of a distant camp fire; to see sustenance in the burr-coated fruit of the *cram cram* bush; to notice the sign posts of day and night, from shifts in sand color to the positions of the moon and stars; and to perceive the security of home in what appears to be a vast wasteland of sand.

For a few weeks some years ago, I stayed in a tiny makeshift village built by nomads on the southern edge of the Sahara. Mat houses were surrounded by slope upon slope of yellow-white sand as far as the eye could see, with occasional clusters of prickly bushes or stunted acacia offering only varying degrees of hopelessness. Still a stranger, I didn't know how to read the desert or her people and I missed my comfortable home. Here, houses appeared ephemeral, vulnerable. Yet curiously, the sense of home within those who built them seemed so solid. It was as if these nomadic herders were literally *homebodies*, carrying all the stuff that home is made of within themselves, able to set it up wherever a bit of grass and water came together for their animals. They seemed to move through the desert not as owners of it, but as travelers ever on a journey to someplace within themselves. It was not an easy journey. But it breathed a graceful perception—for, born of aridity and silence, the nomads survived by responding to their environment, by listening to it and taking careful note of what it had to say.

As my days in their land continued, I noticed that in the stark and simple forever of that space, each living thing pierced by a ray of sunlight took on a significance and wholeness before unfathomed. And at night each cry of delight or sadness resounded from star to star within an enormous arc of darkness.

One evening, the brilliant Pleiades circled overhead like bright-eyed maidens dancing with a young slender moon, while the Milky Way was as the gray halo of age upon the head of that deep blue night. Somewhere in the darkness a pair of hands began to slap a *tam-tam* insistently. Tongues twirled high-pitched screams. Voices chanted. Following the pulse, I came upon a circle of nomads, a sea of dark billowing robes clustered in the sand. Children, bundles of indigo cloth from which pairs of brown feet and tufts of black hair peeked out, stood shoulder to shoulder singing, swaying. Drawn by the music, I joined the circle, watching as everyone sang and danced together in the palm of infinity. All around me the eyes of the robed ones brightly pierced the small, unveiled space between brow and cheek, as if a handful of stars had been tossed at those faces. That community of Tuareg, that small celeste of star-studded robes, echoed the night sky. And I saw a people who were perceptive and pliant partners to their surroundings. They knew how to dance with the moon and the stars.

Sitting there in the desert night, I looked from eye to sky to eye, and suddenly the moon and stars seemed within reach. My own feet began to tap. There in the middle of nowhere was everywhere, and at that moment I was home.

# PLENTY OF ROOM UNDER THE MOON

*For your moon is my moon and my moon is your moon*
*the way we were together together together . . . . is it not lovely?*
~Ric. S. Bastasa

Fongoye, the blacksmith, was going there to cure his brother of alcoholism. Well-schooled in African tradition, he knew his brother's problem was also "his problem." He'd been to see a *marabout,* and the Islamic sage had told him how to help: He gave Fongoye a potion to slip into the brother's beverage—a concoction guaranteed to make the fellow so ill he'd never wish to drink again. However, the holy man said, the potion itself was not enough; to activate the mixture Fongoye would have to slaughter a sheep on the Tuesday and Wednesday prior to using it. So, when he climbed with us into the back of the truck for the two-day drive from Goundam, Mali, in West Africa, to the capital city of Bamako, so did his two sheep.

Dah, an aged and self-appointed civil servant was going to see the President. Not that he'd been invited—but if he did get to see Mali's top statesperson, it wouldn't be his first visit with the man. He'd made a similar journey before to tell

77

him about "local government corruption" in his own town. The President gave him audience, listened attentively, then sent him on his way with sacks of grain and other practical gifts to thank him for his efforts. Now, five years later, carrying new grievances, Dah was determined to see the man again.

Mohamed was going to look for a job at a cigarette factory. One month earlier he'd heard that the factory owner was hiring new workers. Thereafter he'd stuck with our trucker, banking on the fact that in Mali just about every motorized piece of transportation eventually heads to Bamako. He'd banked rightly. At last he was on his way to the capital and his long-awaited job interview. I couldn't help but wonder how old the job news had been when it reached him in the first place.

Although Air Mali (known as "Air Maybe" at the time) flew in and out of Goundam to and from Bamako once a week, I had decided to return to the capital by truck because I wanted to experience Mali on the ground rather than 30,000 feet in the air. I didn't know what I was in for.

I'm not sure why the old Songhai *griot* (traditional oral historian), or the third and fourth sheep, or the other 26 people packed into the back of that truck were going; but they were—*we were*—and we were going together—*very together*.

The first day placed only blazing sun and cloudless sky above our heads and nothing more solid than shifting sand and thorny bushes beneath our wheels. The truck reeled, careened and slid, tossing us about like corn popping in extreme heat. A road it wasn't. Occasional short stretches of smoother clay surface were barely long enough for me to rearrange the duffle bag and grain sacks underneath me.

With every swerve and bump, it seemed as if each person grew in size, and my "territory" became smaller and smaller. The crowd closed in on me until my knees were drawn close to my chest. I felt irritated and frustrated that, for the sake of everyone's comfort, these folks didn't stick to their own spaces. The griot had his damp feet on top of mine; Dah lounged his hairy legs over my ankles; Fongoye stole my best grip location; someone had her knee solid and bony in my back; and a woman's goatskin full of soured milk leaked and dribbled on my arm. I was miserable: hot, gritty, cramped, seared by the merciless sun, longing for the relief of nightfall. To make it all worse, when we hit painfully big bumps or ducked from large, scratching acacia branches everyone *laughed*. "This is funny?" I muttered under my thirsty breath.

Unexpectedly, in the middle of nowhere, we stopped. Something other than gas was in the fuel line, and the driver had to make repairs. Risking what was left of my territory, I cautiously dismounted to stretch my arms and legs. The others, apparently less concerned with ownership than I, tumbled out eagerly, without so much as a backward glance.

Relieved to be standing on the ground in the gracious spaciousness of wide open air, I stretched my hands to the sky and then bent down to touch my toes. Rising back up, I spotted a small caravan of camels ambling through the bush in the distance. Grabbing my camera, I reeled off in their direction, only to be snared by one of countless savage thorn bushes that grumble in the desert sand. Hastily, I unsnagged my skirt and slalomed on through the bramble. Shortly, another nettlesome shrub seized me and the wraparound skirt came loose and fell off. Without stopping, I hoisted it back on, and finally reached shooting distance of the caravan. Lifting my camera, I shot, ran closer; shot again, ran still closer; and then, at just the right spot, pressed the shutter once more—only to find I was out of film. Oh for upcoming days of digital cameras!

I whimper-walked back to our vehicle, and when I got there discovered a colony of tiny burrs on the inside of my skirt. I was standing by the front wheel of the truck plucking them off—growing more perturbed with each pluck—when the griot, who was climbing back into the truck, tumbled into a patch of burrs near my feet. He survived the fall, but his woebegone face announced that he didn't care for those prickly pods any more than I did. I felt a bond with the small fellow as I helped him to his feet. I wondered if this journey would become part of his vast repository of oral traditions—a song of praise or satire about the driver, the truck, the uptight foreigner, or Dah's pilgrimage to see the President?

When the truck was ready, I pulled myself back into the big yellow monster, and soon it was once again bucking and grinding along, drowning out the subtle sounds of the desert. Wearily, still itching and stinging, I picked more burrs from my skirt. Dah helped, and now and then the griot reached over and removed one for me, and I for him. I noticed someone else helping him, too.

It wasn't long after that I felt the griot's sandy, sweaty feet back on top of mine; someone was moving in on what I'd staked out as my new seat; and there was that knee poking into my back again. But I was far too tired to tell them they were invading my domain. Gradually, I stopped fighting the closeness and began to watch how it worked. Each jolt of the truck knitted everyone together a bit more intricately. One could fight the bounces, or be reshaped by them. Most of the others in the truck knew how to roll with the bumps. I'd imagined they were rude and thoughtless to let themselves be jostled into my space; now it occurred to me that they were just adapting. Somehow they knew there was room for all of us, though not necessarily in the places we'd each originally selected for ourselves.

By twilight, all of us were fitting together quite remarkably. Feeling relaxed, I dozed off. When I awoke, the constellations were reciting their bright stories across the sky's indigo stage. The moon shone like a spotlight on our little truck community, and I marveled at what I saw. My feet were stretched over someone's straw basket. A woman was using my legs as a cushion. Dah had fallen asleep, and someone else's arm, in addition to his own, extended out from under his left shoulder. Fongoye's sheep pillowed one another. And Fongoye, except for his head, was buried under the gowns, robes and limbs of several people, snoring contentedly.

Thirty-five creatures, close for comfort.

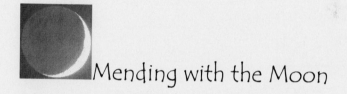 Mending with the Moon

Bunny McBride

# NO MOON

*I love the dark hours of my being.*
*My mind deepens into them.*
*There I can find, as in old letters,*
*The days of my life, already lived,*
*And held like a legend and understood.*
~Rainer Maria Rilke

Regaining consciousness, I became aware of other bodies in other beds. My own body felt terribly alien and frightfully ephemeral. Opening my eyes, I found myself in a dark, strange place, surrounded by an acrid smell. A round light shone through a window pane in what appeared to be a door. At first I thought it was the moon. But no, it was a bare bulb. I struggled to collect my thoughts, to figure out where I was, and why.

I remembered becoming ill with malaria, passing out at an airport, arriving at a friend's house, and him placing me in a bed there. I had a vague sense of him sleeping on the floor beside that bed—keeping vigil through the night, I later learned. Foggy headed and desperately tired, I had yearned for sleep. But every time I closed my eyes, the hallucination came: a congregation of holy men gathered around me, calling the community to prayer and chanting Koranic scriptures. The only way to quiet the distracting din was to open my eyes. When I did, the crowd disappeared. But each time I lowered my lids, the robed men returned and kept me awake. I wondered why my friend didn't ask them to leave.

By dawn, listless and delusional, I had a profound yearning to let go of life altogether. In my imagination, I saw myself clinging to a thick rope hanging from the sky. My hands ached. I couldn't bear holding on any longer. Letting go, I felt the rope slipping through my hands as I plummeted downward. It was such a relief. As I slid, I murmured, "Ahhh, yes . . ."

Then, suddenly, I thought, "NO!" Grabbing the rope I'd conjured in my mind, I whispered the name of my photographer friend with whom I'd been traveling in the West African country of Mali to document the lives of nomads living on the southern edge of the Sahara. Immediately he was at my bedside. Perhaps he had been there all along. Pulling out a notepad, he said, "We're going to make a list of everything you're grateful for in life. Everything you want to live for." Later I learned that what seemed to me like a few minutes' task continued for some two hours. Then I drifted away again. When I came to I was in that dark space with the acrid smell and the false moon. At that moment, I didn't realize it was the intensive care unit of a hospital in Dakar, Senegal. And I didn't know that on top of malaria, I had hepatitis.

Disoriented and striving to get my bearings, I tried to pray, but couldn't put together a single phrase in my head. With thoughts floundering, I became aware of a woman two beds over from me. I could hear her whimpering and moaning, an awful, hopeless wail. Focusing on her, I heard myself speak, trying to stop the crying and offer some comfort. I think my halting words to her were the answer to my unuttered prayer for myself, because every effort I made on her behalf consoled me. For a long time, I'd known that we grow stronger reaching out to others, but that night I felt as if it saved my life.

Daylight brought my photographer friend to the room. He had a letter for me from my then husband, who had moved from our east coast home to California for a year-long journalism fellowship. Aware that my husband had begun to question whether he wanted to return to me and our life together in Boston, my friend hesitated before asking if I'd like him to read me the letter. I wanted to hear it, but it was bad news—bad enough to make me question whether I wanted to get well and continue life.

After two weeks, encouraged by my work partner's daily visits, messages and prayers from family, and the warm mellow voice of an African friend who helped sing me to life with traditional Wolof songs, I felt anxious to go home. Despite objections from the doctors, I checked out of the hospital and with the help of friends made it to the airport. Brought to the plane in a wheelchair, I slept the entire flight, laid out across three seats. When I was wheeled off the plane in New York, my own sister didn't recognize me. After a shaky week at the home of my photographer friend's parents, I was taken to my parents' home where I spent another month recuperating. Then, at last, I went back to my own place in Boston.

Soon after my return, my long hair began falling out in fistfuls. When I walked down the street, it flew from my head. Combing it in front of the bathroom mirror each morning, I filled the sink with a tumble of blond strands. Troubled by the loss, I stopped combing. When a friend who had been in the Peace Corps stopped by for a visit, I greeted her wearing a scarf wrapped around my head. She commented on it. I explained, and she said that she, too, had experienced hair loss after being treated for malaria. She went back to her place and retrieved what was left of the medicine she'd been prescribed as an antidote.

After placing the small bottle in my hands, she left. I opened it, then paused and put the lid back on. Unsettled by the idea of taking one drug to adjust the side effects of another, I went out for a walk to think things through. Round and round my city block I went, eyes down, thought turned inward. In searching mode, I sang softly to myself the first verse of an old hymn, repeating it many times as I walked:

Trust the Eternal when the shadows gather
When joys of daylight seem so like a dream.
God the unchanging pities like a father.
Trust on and wait your daystar yet shall gleam.

I was in my own world and had no interest in talking with anyone. Yet, when I passed an acquaintance who was sitting on her stoop a few doors down from my home, I felt impelled to stop. The woman was a child psychiatrist, and a minute or two into our brief talk, I found myself asking her if she used drugs to treat the children who came under her care.

"Yes," she answered.

"Do they have side effects?"

"Yes."

"Do they heal?"

Here she paused before saying, "No, but they help with the symptoms."

"How do you decide whether to give them?" I asked.

"It all depends on what the goal is, what is most important. For example, if parents come to me with a hyperactive child and the goal is to quiet hyperactivity and improve attentiveness, they often decide that using a drug to reach that goal is worthwhile, even though it may make their child nauseous, anxious, or dizzy."

As I walked away, one thought rang in my head: "It all depends on what the goal is, what is most important." I realized that my most important goal was not to get back my hair or even my husband. What I really wanted was an inner equanimity so profound that no external disturbance—be it betrayal or a disease-carrying bug—could shake it.

Serenity of spirit became my goal. I decided not to take the antidote. Having lost about two-thirds of my hair, I cut the rest quite short. Then, over the next two months I split my days in half—spending the mornings in prayer, meditation, and spiritual research, and the afternoons doing my writing work. During that time a mass of tiny new hairs sprouted up all over my scalp. More important, I found a sense of peace that ultimately made it possible to let my husband go with grace. Although others called it a "divorce," I called it a renaissance—a rebirth of our marriage relationship into a friendship that continues to this day.

Shortly after talking with the child psychiatrist on her front stoop, I moved out of town. Five years later, after going to graduate school in New York and relocating in Maine, I ran into her at a party while visiting old friends in Boston.

Seeing each other across the room, we made a beeline toward one another. Coming face to face, both of us said essentially the same thing: "I've wanted to thank you for five years." It was then I learned that on the day our paths crossed, she had also been troubled and was sitting on her stoop contemplating her life's purpose. To my great surprise, she told me, "When you asked me if prescribing drugs to children healed them and I had to answer no, I realized that healing was what I wanted to do with my life. For years I had thought about becoming a minister. Our brief talk helped me make that decision. I quit my job, went to seminary, and now have my own congregation."

And so it was that in the middle of a party five years after a dark day, both of us made a discovery: Even when we feel so burdened that it seems we can barely help ourselves, the simple act of heartfelt searching may inspire those who cross our path—and actually bring them to our path.

# HOW EASILY MENDS THE MOON

*Thirst drove me down to the water,*
*where I drank the moon's reflection.* ~Rumi

I awoke squirming and scratching. The sun was already up, slanting through my window, announcing a bright spring day. But I felt terrible, itchy from head to toe. Throwing back the covers, I saw a rash running the length of my arms and legs and spilling onto my hands and feet.

I grew up with parents who followed a particular mind/body practice long before the term became so popular. Their first response to physical, social, and professional problems was prayer. To their way of thinking, prayer was not about trying to get God's attention and begging for help. Rather it was about tuning in to a divine order of being and trying to align their thoughts and actions with that—with what they referred to as the universal Principle of wholeness, balance, and wellbeing.

Echoing their tradition, I tried to collect my thoughts, to replace feelings of irritation (in all senses of the word) with the idea of balanced being. If this bothersome breakout was the result of some mental aggravation, I wanted to meet it right there at the root of the problem.

All morning long I sought relief in this kind of mindfulness, in vain. I was so distracted by my prickled skin that I couldn't bring a single thought into focus for more than a few seconds. I tried to steer my consciousness toward the divine by making a mental gratitude list. Before making much headway on that, I found myself busy rearranging the bedding in an effort to get comfortable. I started again, only to have my thought trail off as I got up to open a window. And again, as I felt pulled to the kitchen to brew a cup of tea. And again . . . and again . . . By 2pm, I had pursued countless short-term diversions from my discomfort, but had not come close to escaping it.

I decided to phone my sister, who had helped me work through a wide variety of challenges with prayer. I don't remember exactly what she said, but she quieted my anxious thoughts and stirred hope with a promise to pray for me. Weary, I went to the couch and lay down on my back, tucking my hands under my bottom to keep myself from scratching. My husband came in with a fresh cup of steaming tea and sat down beside me. He's an agnostic, but open-minded and supportive of my spiritual approach to wellness. He's also a non-alarmist, let-the-problem-run-its-course kind of guy who rarely seeks medical help for himself. So, he was compassionate, not worried. He was also curious.

"So what is this?" he asked, and then ventured several answers to his own question:

"Do you think you got into some poison ivy when we pulled our canoe up on the island yesterday and wandered through the woods? Or maybe you're allergic to that new kind of fish we ate last night? Or is this a stress reaction to the horrible news of your friend's death. Or . . ."

While musing on all of these possibilities, he caressed my brow with his palm. I sighed, grateful for his care—and for the distraction. Then something occurred to me: All of the possible causes he mentioned were reasonable explanations on a purely physical plane. Yet, I wasn't looking for material causes and antidotes. My deepest desire was for a spiritual insight that would enable me to transcend the problem. With this thought, I fell asleep.

Waking up to the sound of the phone ringing, I heard my husband answer and say playfully, "Whatever you're doing, it's not working." Then he paused, listening for a few moments before bringing the phone to me. "Be happy. It's your sister."

"I'm calling to tell you it *is* working," she laughed. She recounted some of the ideas that had come to her during her prayer and meditation on my behalf. In short: She saw me whole and felt confident that I was so.

"But I still itch like mad," I complained. She told me that no matter what I was experiencing, my fundamental wholeness was intact and that she felt sure I would soon realize that. "Just rest in that idea and let go of anxiousness," she said.

Clicking off the phone, I handed it to my husband with a half-hearted smile and a comment about being blessed with a wonderful sister even though her instruction to let go of anxiousness seemed a tall order.

"Yes, you are blessed," he said, adding, "and now, get up and get dressed. You've been inside all day feeling miserable. It's time for some fresh air and a walk."

I protested, but he pulled me up, told me I'd be glad once we were outside, and sent me into the bedroom to get dressed.

It was an extraordinary spring night. Blue-black sky, brilliant full moon, air fresh as ginger ale. Strolling along the river behind our home, we came to the town's boat landing and walked to the outer edge of the dock. Standing there, leaning against my husband, I drank in the stillness and sighed. Then I noticed two moons: one in the sky above, the other exquisitely reflected in the glistening black water. The river, skimming quietly along its bed in the breathless night, was a mirror.

We stood there for quite some time without saying a word. Then, suddenly, a gust of wind swept through the scene, cooling my face and ruffling the water. In an instant, the river moon broke into thousands of pieces. It was so startling that I glanced at the moon above, half expecting to see it shattered. But it remained intact—fat, round, and radiant. Almost as quickly as the wind came, it disappeared. The water quieted and its moon pieced back together.

"Wow," I whispered. "I just saw my haiku."

"What do you mean?" he asked.

"In my blue journal, the one that came with a poem on every page, there's a haiku by 'anonymous' that I loved the moment I read it, even though I wasn't sure what it meant. It goes like this:

> Broken and broken
> again on the wave
> how easily mends the moon"

Back home, nestled in bed for the night, I thought about the haiku and what I'd just seen. All it took was calmness to restore the reflected moon to the wholeness of the original. In quietness, the river had received the fully intact image of that luminous orb. In turmoil, she'd lost it. In stillness, she'd found it anew. All day long, anxiety had accompanied my discomfort. In the back of my mind I'd worried, *What is this? Will it get worse? Will it spread to my face? How long will it last?* But now, picturing the graceful reassembling of the moon in the river, the river of my mind quieted and my worries faded. I recalled the line about the shepherd in the 23rd Psalm—"He leads me beside still waters"—and it took on new meaning for me: *Still waters, clear reflection.* I pictured still waters in countless forms and sizes, all reflecting the same moon—deep rivers, quiet coves, deltas, lakes, ponds, pools, puddles, dewdrops. Words can't capture the feeling I had at that moment, but it was a profound sense that I was no more or less than a reflection or emanation of the divine order of being—that universal Principle of wholeness, balance, and wellbeing.

All anxiety gone, I slept peacefully that night. Come morning, the rash was gone. Would it have disappeared without my sister's prayers or the experience of seeing the moon mending? Perhaps, but I would have missed the epiphany on reflection. It was a moment of clarity and grace that I've called to memory time and time again. It always calms my thought, clears my mind of unhealthy distractions, and awakens a sense of my spiritual essence, ever intact.

## MOON DATES

*I wake and spend the last hours of darkness*
*with no one but the moon.*
*She listens . . . and comforts me surely with her light.*

~Mary Oliver

I married a traveler. So did my husband. Sometimes we go together, but often we head out on our own for research and writing purposes or to give a talk here or there. When only one of us is leaving, we begin the parting with a card. Whoever is staying behind slips it into the other's travel bag. The one who's leaving puts their message somewhere in the house where it's certain to be found—on the kitchen counter, atop a bed pillow, or leaning against the bathroom mirror.

Over several decades this written "fare well" practice has become a treasured tradition. When I'm the one who has left the sweet familiarity of home, I force myself to wait until I've reached my destination before looking for the card tucked among the clothes in my suitcase. Wherever I'm sleeping that first night in a new place—in hotel, hut, or tent—I retrieve the note, prop myself up on one elbow and read my husband's words. Sometimes romantic, other times encouraging, comforting, or endearingly silly, they always connect me to home and remind me that I am loved. Typically, I reread his message every night before going to bed. By the time I return home, I usually know it by heart.

During long journeys of several weeks or months, we write additional letters or call. But when traveling in remote places that make that difficult or impossible, we have "moon dates"—moments when we find the moon in our respective skies and use her as a sort of go-between. There's something wondrous about looking up at that heavenly light and knowing that someone dear to you is doing the same at that very moment in another corner of the world. It's a tangible, sometimes palpable, connection. And the way the moon appears to follow both of you simultaneously if you walk during your long distance date seems nothing short of magic.

The idea for moon dates came from a song I learned at summer camp many years ago:

I see the moon and the moon sees me.
The moon sees somebody I'd like to see.
God bless the moon and God bless me,
And God bless somebody I'd like to see.

There were many moon dates in the Spring of 1997, when my husband traveled to remote areas in Bolivia, Brazil, and Paraguay for two months to visit the Bororo, Ayoreo, Nambikwara, and several other indigenous groups with unpronounceable names. He went without a satellite phone or any other telecommunication devices. Knowing that he would have few opportunities to call or send a letter, I checked the moonrise/moonset charts, looking for moments when we could both see the moon. At first, timing seemed important, but after a while that ceased to matter. I found myself looking for the moon at random moments. Whenever I saw it, I paused to think of my partner, sending him love and good thoughts, and whispering a bit of news. I sensed he was doing the same. Weeks went by without a letter or a call, other than the initial "I landed safely" call at the beginning of his trip when his plane arrived in Paraguay's capital city, Asuncion.

Then, out of the blue, about five weeks into his journey, a ringing phone woke me from a deep sleep. Opening my eyes, I saw that it was still dark. Picking up the phone, I glanced at the clock. Almost 4:30 a.m.

"Hello?"

"Bun?"

"Yes . . . Who is this—Harald?!

"Yes."

Immediately I'm wide awake. Celebratory. "You found a phone. Where are you? I'm so happy you're calling!

I've missed you, and thought of you countless times –

"I'm glad to hear that because I need you. I'm having some trouble . . ."

Suddenly I'm still. Alert. In listening mode. "What's going on?"

"I'm in Bolivia. In Cochabamba. At one of those public phones on the street."

His voice is odd, halting. "I came down with something in the bush. Probably amoebic dysentery. Felt lousy on the long bus ride from Vallegrande to Cochabamba. At a pharmacy next to the bus station I got some drug that was supposed to help, but things only got worse. I've been hallucinating. I feel disoriented. Dizzy. Nervous."

He has never said anything like this to me before. In all our years together, I've never seen him really worried. He's the most fearless and resilient person I know. More than the rotten symptoms of dysentery, I'm concerned about the confusion in his head. Searching for the right words, I respond slowly, thoughtfully: "Yesterday I read something about the concept of atonement as 'oneness of being.' The author divided the syllables of the word as *at-one-ment*. You know how close we feel to each other, even when far apart?

"Yes."

"Well, even closer than that is your nearness to the divine source of your being. You are inseparable from that.

You are the very emanation of the Life Force. I call it God, but the name doesn't matter. It's your lifeline." I want to illustrate this by reaching across the miles and taking his hand. Since that's impossible, I say, "Can you do something for me?"

"Ok."

"Keep this one idea in mind: *at-one-ment*. Hold to it and know that I'm always thinking of you, supporting and loving you across the miles, just as – " He cuts me off:

"I will. I can't talk anymore. I'm light headed. It's hard to concentrate. I have to go. I love you."

And just like that, he was gone. By now my eyes were accustomed to the darkness. I noticed moonlight angling through the window. From my bed, I couldn't see the moon itself, but I knew it was nearly full and about to set—as it had already done in Bolivia two hours ahead of my time zone. So I closed my eyes and pictured the light of dawn shining on my life partner.

My day was filled with teaching classes and meeting with students in my office, but every time he came to mind, I pictured him feeling loved, whole, and at peace. Quakers refer to this kind of thinking as "holding someone in the light." Rather than focusing on a problem—an illness, weakness, setback, or fear—you see them surrounded by love and light, illuminating their core completeness, strength, and resilience.

The next morning, the phone rang at 6. It was Harald again. He had stopped taking what he called the "suspicious horse-cure." The psychotic feelings had passed, but he still felt ill—his misery compounded by being alone in a strange city without a single contact. As he told me about that, I remembered something from an essay on solitude written by my old Australian writing teacher:

"You're not really alone," I said. "When you feel that way, try saying the word another way: 'al(l) one.' One with me. One with Life. One with the source of all life."

"All one," he repeated, as if saying a prayer. Then he told me he had found a gastroenterological specialist and was going there after talking with me. "Mostly," he said, I'm calling to thank you for your help. A few hours after our talk yesterday, I sensed I had turned the corner. Whatever you're doing, I feel the embrace of your thoughts. . . ."

Over the next two weeks, as the moon passed through its phases from full to last quarter to waning crescent, I heard nothing more from South America. Since I couldn't call or write my husband, I talked to the moon. On night walks, I imagined that the moon shadow following me was not my own, but my husband's. When the orb was luminously full, I saw it as a light at the end of a tunnel. Whatever its shape or brightness, I took comfort in picturing it shining on him. But then, reaching "new" phase, it turned dark and, like my partner, disappeared. It was an act of faith to know that both of them were intact and moving gracefully through their proper orbits.

Finally, when the moon reappeared as a slender waxing crescent, a long letter from my husband arrived in the mail, dated the day after our last phone talk. It said, in part:

> After our last talk, I saw the gastroenterological specialist. His immediate diagnosis matched mine, intestinal amoebas, and he took blood and stool samples. But the next day, the test results were all negative, despite the clarity of the symptoms. This really surprised him, and me too. Perhaps the medicine did work its share before I stopped taking it, but I attribute the improvement primarily to your help. So, I'm ready for the next leg of my trip, which I didn't have to cancel for health reasons after all!
>
> What I've (re-)learned through this is how significant it is to know that we're not alone, but, as you say it, all-one. Your most helpful thought was *at-one-ment*. I repeated it every time I needed to focus my mind and not become distracted by the noise and visual overdose all around me. I'll keep that word, that concept, in mind.

Anyway, this quick note is to thank you from the depth of my heart, a special place where I keep my treasures, in particular my love for you.

Your life-mate,

Harald

And this essay is my thank-you to the moon for the solace it offered while I awaited this news. Its shining presence reassured me that both of us are held in the Light.

# PASSING ON

*As bees gather honey,*
*so we collect what is sweetest out of all things and build.*
~Rainer Maria Rilke

"Should I come now?" I asked my father over the phone. "It's no problem to change my flight and I would love to join you alongside Mom sooner rather than later." She had been in a nursing home for seven days. It was hard to picture her there, a stalwart 83-year-old woman who had taken up running at age 70, announcing that she hadn't been strong enough to do so earlier.

"No, honey, everything's okay," my father responded. "We don't want to give your mother the feeling that we're all rushing to her death bed. Keep your Monday flight. Your arrival will be something for her to look forward to." He was certain she would rally and be well, for that's how it had always been.

So I waited. An hour before getting into the car for the long drive to the airport, I received a call from the head nurse. My mother had passed on. I was stunned. All the more so when the nurse asked if I would like to speak with her.

"What? Speak with my mother?"

Gently, she explained the offer: "It's said that hearing and consciousness continue for a time even after vital life signs are no longer evident."

"Really?"

"Yes. If you'd like to talk to her, I'll go to her room and ring you back from there in about five minutes. Okay?"

"Okay." Five minutes to think about the last thing I would say to the woman whose vibrant love for life in general and family in particular had surrounded me for as long as I could remember . . .

The same year my mother took up running, she formalized her work as a spiritual practitioner, committing herself to helping people deal with all kinds of problems through prayerful meditation. The spiritual thread in her life had been a constant, but it had woven through a series of professions and avocations—piano performance and teaching, deeply involved motherhood, high level computer programming and systems analysis, fund raising for music schools and symphonies, and caring for her elderly parents. In addition, after becoming a practitioner, she gave occasional lectures on her spiritual research. She believed one could "do it all," but not all at once. So she lived her life in chapters, each one distinctly full. She was not a woman without flaws, but she had many gifts and put them to use with enormous energy and an eye to helping others.

On that January day when Mom passed on, my plane to DC lifted off at sunset. I leaned my head against the cold window and watched the sky turn dark. Closing my eyes, I thought about the last words I said to her as the nurse held the phone to her ear: I had poured out a soliloquy of gratitude for all the good she had brought into my life. The list included joy, music, discipline and just demands, a vibrant and consistent love, and most of all a spiritual foundation. As I spoke about these things, I heard myself shift from giving thanks to offering a promise that I would strive to honor everything worthwhile that I'd learned through her by living it in my own life. At that moment, Mom's passing on did an about face and took on new meaning. Beyond the transition from one plane of being to another, her passing was a moment in time to carefully note the good that she had "passed on" to me. To make that my own.

Opening my eyes, what did I see out the window but the moon, staring straight at me as if it had sought me out. It followed the plane like a mother's heart, transforming the black night. Wide-eyed, I returned its gaze for the rest of the flight, until it slipped from sight when the pilot turned toward the airport to land.

Two years later, at a fancy party following an exhibit opening at the Q'uai Branley Museum in Paris, I met a French neurologist. It was a mild autumn night and we were on the deck of a boat tethered to the bank of the Seine River near the museum. Our conversation roamed through a range of topics and ideas, but one question churned in the back of my mind: *Was it true, what the nurse told me about hearing and consciousness continuing for a time after a person's vital signs are gone?* I yearned to ask him. But I was also afraid that his answer would steal the comfort I'd found in believing it.

Curiosity won out. I asked. He told me that hearing is the last of the senses to be lost in the death process and that it persists even when the person is unconscious, in a coma, or otherwise not responsive.

"But," I pressed, "does it continue after the vital signs are gone?"

"We don't know for sure," he said, but studies of people who have been revived after going through the death experience suggest that may be true."

Perhaps he was just being gentle with me, aware of the circumstances behind my question. But I now realize that even if his answer had been "Absolutely not," it wouldn't matter. When someone dies, those of us who love them can search for ways to keep the goodness, strengths, and lessons of that life alive. By noting, living, and passing on the positive habits of being embodied in a loved one, we maintain their company. This eases the missing and allows the message of that life to continue its sweet influence. And if parts of the package are not worthy of being passed on? May those be cast aside while we devote ourselves to building with the honey gathered in our hearts.

Bunny McBride

# SOARING

*Sorrow sweeps everything out of your house,*

*so that new joy can find space to enter.* ~Rumi

I grew up certain that no one could play Robert Schumann's "Soaring" (Op. 12 no. 2) on the piano better than my mother. Schumann conceived the piece as a depiction of the character Florestan in Beethoven's opera, *Fidelio.* A political prisoner sentenced to death, Florestan is rescued by his wife Lenore who disguises herself as a guard. Of course, I didn't know this as a child. Nor did I read notes about the composition, such as this one:

> "Soaring," is a powerful treatment of the idea of human ambition, mounting with irresistible, inherent strength toward the summits of fame and achievement, scorning obstacles, defying dangers, ignoring temptations and the soft allurements of easier paths; sweeping onward with the overwhelming force of a tidal wave toward its goal, grand but destructive in its might.

While I can easily picture my mother rescuing my father like Lenore rescued Florestan, the emotional interpretation quoted above is a far cry from what I felt when listening to her rendition of the piece. To me, "Soaring" was an irresistibly wild burst of energy that matched her zest for life. When she played it, one paid attention. One could imagine leaves on the trees outside our living room window turning to an upright position at her opening salvo and colliding in thunderous applause when she finished. The primary emotion it stirred in me was pure *joy*, which, quite fittingly, was one of my father's two nicknames for Mom. (The other was "Button," because of her petite nose.)

Although my mother majored in music at Cornell University and attended Julliard summer school, she had no aspirations to become a concert pianist. That dream belonged to her mother, who imposed a strict 4-hours-a-day practice schedule on both of her daughters. There were two grand pianos in their home, one of them in my grandmother's art studio. While painting, she would call out instructions: "*forte*, not *pianissimo*!" or, "B *flat*, can't you hear that?!" Mom and her sister sometimes bribed one another for reprieve from being the one to practice in the studio.

My mother performed vespers while attending Cornell and while teaching music at New York's Knox School for girls, known for its rich music and art programs. She gave several concerts there and in Washington, DC, after marrying, but when motherhood came her way, she was pleased to leave the stage. As it turned out, what she loved most was *listening* to music, and she did that with even more gusto than she played. She'd lower her eyelids, lift her head, and sway with the melody. Sometimes she hummed along. I'd look at my sister and we'd roll our eyes. But we didn't really mind, unless we were at a concert or with friends being chauffeured by Mom while she listened to the classical radio station.

Mom made sure that we grew up surrounded by music. She bought tickets to the symphony and other musical events that we attended as a family. She gave us our first piano lessons, before handing us over to another teacher. She also required us to learn a second instrument—flute for me, clarinet for my sister. Aware that her daughters had no performance aspirations, she was satisfied with an hour's practice a day on the piano and half an hour on our "other" instrument. For two summers in our early teens, she signed us up for summer orchestra—not how we'd pictured ourselves spending our mornings during the warm months. One day, driving us to the local high school for these thrice weekly sessions, she got caught up in some classical piece. Her head swayed as she hummed with the radio. She must have kept her eyes open—she was driving, after all—but in her fervor she missed the turn to the school. She turned around and took another pass at it. But the music was swelling and she missed it again. One more failed attempt and she announced, laughing, "Well girls, now we're too late. I'm afraid you'll have to miss orchestra today." No eye rolling that morning; my sister and I exchanged gleeful smiles.

Fifty years and countless musical events later, Mom passed away quite suddenly. It happened on a Monday. On Tuesday, my sister and I talked Dad into making a reservation for Wednesday high tea and music at the Strathmore Mansion near their home. It was something Mom loved to do. And I felt certain it was something she would have suggested if she could. We went, hoping that listening to the pianist who was performing that day would lift our spirits. As it turned out, we were all too numb for that to happen.

After two weeks with our father, my sister and I had to return to our own homes. Leaving Dad alone for the first time was nearly as heartbreaking as realizing that Mom, our dear "Joy," was gone. Just before heading to the airport, I went to her study to get the boarding pass I'd printed the previous night. Noticing her portable CD player on one of the shelves, I wondered what the last piece of music was that she had listened to. I lifted the lid to see if it held a disk. It did. I didn't have my reading glasses handy, so couldn't quite read the label, except to see that it was something by Brahms. I decided to take it home with me, for later listening. I opened mom's CD drawer, found an empty Brahms case lying on top of the stack, and slipped the disk into it.

By the time my connecting flight landed at the local airport, it was dark. A cold February night with two bits of comfort: the friend who picked me up and the lovely half-moon that followed us home. Somehow knowing that I didn't feel like visiting, my friend kissed me goodbye in the driveway, gave me a still-warm loaf of her homemade banana bread, and waited to drive off until I was safely in the house.

My husband was still at the university, in the middle of teaching his once-a-week, 3-hour class, so I was home alone. He had laid a fire to keep me company. I lit it and made myself a cup of tea. On the kitchen counter, I found a stack of mail that had arrived while I was away—condolence cards. Carrying them and my cup to the living room, I sat down by the fire intending to read. Instead, I stared blankly at the flames while the scent of burning cedar filled the room. After a while, remembering the CD I'd brought from Mom's study, I retrieved it, wanting to hear something I knew she had listened to recently. Then, slipping on my reading glasses, I discovered what her last song had been: Brahms' *Requiem*.

"Oh no!," I said out loud, taken by surprise and troubled to think that she had been listening to music composed for death without having hinted to any of us that she thought her end might be near. Feeling wary but irresistibly drawn to the music, I placed the disk into the player, leaned back in the chair, and closed my eyes. As the music swelled, filled with the human sorrow that pours over us in the face of death, I wept.

But then, something remarkable happened. In the 4th movement the tone shifted from dark and heavy to light and tranquil, as if window curtains had been opened just when the first sliver of dawn showed itself on the horizon. And then, in the 5th movement, dawn *arrived*, absolutely FULL of light and love and comfort. When it ended, I opened the CD cover to see if there was a translation of the German. This is what I found:

*Ye now have sorrow, but I will*
*see you again, and your heart*
*shall rejoice, and your joy*
*no man taketh from you.*

(John 16:22)

*I will comfort you as one whom his*
*Mother comforteth*

(Isaiah 66:13)

*Behold me with your eyes: a little*
*while I have had tribulation and labor,*
*and now have found great comfort.*

(Ecclesiastes 51:35)

It was as if Mom had left a message for my sister and me to find—that joy is powerful, a mother's comforting love is eternal, and tribulation passes. That this message came in music, the form of artful expression she had treasured above all others, made it shine with a brilliance I can't begin to describe. I wept all over again—but this time I felt as if my tears were washing away sorrow.

Reading the rest of the music notes that came with the CD, I discovered that Brahms wrote this requiem for his mother. While composing, did he, like me, cross the bridge of sorrow to celebrate a mother's life and claim her presence in a new and lasting way?

Bunny McBride

## DEEP BREATHING

*The moon filled and overflowed the night with revelations of her light.*
~ Henry Wadsworth Longfellow

The night our mother died, my sister and I climbed into our parents' big bed with our father. Still shaken by the loss, none of us even considered spending the night alone. We lay there on our backs, three bereaved souls in a row, staring up into the darkness. "I don't think I can sleep at all," said Dad, who had shared a bed with Mom for nearly 60 years. My sister assured him that he could. "We're all exhausted," she said gently, "and rest will be a sweet relief. Let's do some deep breathing together to help us let go of the day." Then she guided us into that much needed realm of slumber.

Nearly every night thereafter, for the next four years, either my sister or I put our father to bed this way, sometimes in person, often over the phone. His bedtime was usually around 10:30 p.m. If we hadn't talked earlier, we'd fill each other in on the day's doings. Almost invariably, this included Dad asking, "What was your highlight today?" After listening to mine, he'd share his. That's how he handled grief—continually looking for something bright amid the shadows.

Whenever I visited him at his home in the outskirts of Washington, DC, the highlight he mentioned always involved something simple we'd done together: taking a walk on the Trolley Trail, talking over morning coffee and pastry at his favorite French café, watching dogs being groomed at the local PetCo, eating the "fantastic" dinner I prepared, or sitting together on the couch in the TV room looking at an old movie classic such as "It's a Wonderful Life" or something slightly more recent that captured his fancy, such as Woody Allen's "Radio Days."

My sister and I had very similar deep breathing narratives, aiming to keep them comfortingly familiar for Dad. But we nuanced our lines here and there, including adjusting our nightly descriptions of the moon. Typically, after talking about the highlights of our day, I would say, "Okay, it's time to begin moving toward sleep. Let's start by closing our eyes and taking one giant breath: In . . . and out." Then I'd continue like this:

> Let's gather up any distracting thoughts that might keep us from sleep, all thoughts concerning the past, present, and future, and place them in a big brown paper bag. . . . Now, reach in deeper and pull out the last vestiges of those thoughts, especially anything having to do

with tomorrow, trusting that everything you need to know will come to you fresh and new right when you need it. And now, with all thoughts in the bag, let's tie it up, hook it to a great balloon, and set it free out the window. There it goes, rising toward a luminous moon that is nearly full and already so high in tonight's clear sky. A light wind comes along and carries the balloon higher. Another breeze moves it across the face of the moon. And one more takes it beyond the moon and out of sight. Once out of sight, it is also out of mind, as are all the thoughts that it's carrying. There's nothing left but a wide open space, full of grace. And in that place we greet our sleep by breathing in, then out.

After each long inhale and exhale, my father would count, "That's one . . . that's two . . ." all the way up to ten. Then, our counting done, he'd say, "And now, we'll sleep the whole night through." If I was at his home, I'd kiss him on the cheek and head to the guestroom. As I closed his door, he'd call out sleepily, "Thank you, honey. I love you so much. See you in the morning!"

Sometimes he did not sleep the whole night through. Hearing him up and about, I'd get out of bed to make sure that all was well. Often I'd find him standing in his pajamas on the balcony, holding a cup of hot chocolate and gazing at the moon. Rather than complain about not being able to sleep, he'd offer me a sip and talk about the moon's beauty as if he were seeing it for the first time. Clearly, I'm my father's daughter in this regard.

On nights when my sister and I were both out with friends, out of the country, or otherwise occupied, whichever one of us was more easily interruptible made the night phone call to dad—sometimes slipping away from a movie theater or a dining table for a few minutes in order to ring him. Some of our friends admired this, while others thought we were carrying daughterly duty way too far. But for us, it always felt like love, not duty. Our memories were full of countless childhood nights when Dad had put us to bed with stories he made up especially for us. Hot summer nights when he would slip into our room to raise the windows higher and tie back the curtains so the night breeze could fly our way. Cool autumn nights when he'd wake us up and lead us outside to look at our carved Halloween pumpkins lit and glowing in the windows. As we saw it, phoning him at bedtime barely called up the balance to his fatherly care.

Occasionally, however, we worried that we might be robbing Dad of the ability to fall asleep unaided. So after three and a half years, we suggested skipping deep breathing on Sunday nights. One Monday morning, about a month into this new plan, I found this voice mail from him on my phone:

> Well, hi Bunny! I know this is your Sunday night holiday from deep breathing. It's now just about 9 o'clock here and 8 o'clock there. I'm not calling for deep breathing, but to just give you a report on today's activities in case there's anything to report that you'd like to hear or don't know, and to see what's going on with you. But I'm not calling for Sunday night deep breathing, because there is none, right? (chuckle). Maybe we'll 'touch base,' as you say, in just a little bit. I love you. Goodbye for now.

After that, we resumed Sunday night calls. I'm grateful for that because, as it turned out, Dad's life did not continue for very many more Sundays.

Sitting beside him during his sudden and short stay in a nursing home, my sister and I held his hands, stroked his brow, and reminisced about our lives together. After briefly opening his eyes and saying "Ahhh!" when we first arrived at his bedside together, he had not communicated with us for three days. But we took some comfort in his apparent tranquility. His head rested easily on the two pillows that framed his face, still handsome in his ninth decade. He breathed softly and peacefully. Then, all of sudden, he had a bout of hiccups so intense that they shook his entire body. Five minutes passed. Then ten. He seemed to be gasping for breath. Then I remembered our deep breathing tradition. So I began, "You are my highlight, Dad. . . . And now, let's gather up any distracting thoughts that may be keeping you from rest. Let's put them in the big brown bag, tie it up, hook it to the great balloon, and set it free out the window. There it goes, rising up toward the luminous moon . . . moving beyond the moon and out of sight. . . . Nothing is left but a wide open space, full of grace—the perfect place to welcome rest by breathing in, then out." I counted the breaths since Dad could not. By the time I reached ten, he was breathing peacefully again. This happened several more times that day—and then he took his last breath.

Now, when I see the moon shining at night, I picture a balloon gliding across its face, carrying my father's thoughts. And I hear Dad asking, "What was your highlight today?"

# ABOUT THE AUTHOR

Bunny McBride is an award winning author and veteran traveler who writes most often about cultural survival and wildlife conservation. She has written for international newspapers and magazines about Chinese people in the aftermath of the communist Cultural Revolution, Tuareg camel nomads in the Sahara, threatened gorillas in Rwanda and lemurs in Madagascar, Sami reindeer herders in arctic Scandinavia, Maasai cattle herders in East Africa, and Mi'kmaq basketmakers in Aroostook County, Maine. Her books include *Women of the Dawn, Molly Spotted Elk: A Penobscot in Paris,* and *Our Lives in Our Hands: Micmac Indian Basketmakers.* Co-authored titles include *Indians in Eden, Asticou's Island Domain, The Audubon Field Guide to African Wildlife,* and multiple editions of the textbook *Cultural Anthropology: The Human Challenge.* She holds an MA in Anthropology from Columbia University.

WITHDRAWN

main
9.95

WITHDRAWN

29499333R00084

Made in the USA
Charleston, SC
13 May 2014